ACC. No. 74/013208 CLASS No. 759.06 M

MID-CHESHIRE CENTRAL COLLEGE

BK04720 OF

FURTHER EDUCATION, HARTFORD, NORTHWICH

KT-237-250

This book is due for return on or before the last date shown below.

07 MAY 2002	-4 NOV 2005
05 JUL 2002	-3 JUL 2006
-1 NOV 2002	-5 MAR 2007
22 NOV 2002	15 DEC 2008
12 Dec 02	-3 FEB 2009
21 OCT 2003	-5 MAR 2009
-3 FEB 2004	05 NOV 2010
	26 NOV 2010
05 JAN 2005	-5 OCT 2012
14 APR 2005	

Don Gresswell Ltd., London, N21 Cat. No. 1207

DG 02242/71

BK04720

MATISSE

MATISSE

by
Gérard Durozoi

BRACKEN BOOKS

LONDON

Originally published by Fernand Hazan, Paris 1989

Translation into English by John Greaves

This edition published 1989 by Bracken Books
an imprint of Bestseller Publications Ltd
Princess House, 50 Eastcastle Street
London W1N 7AP, England

Copyright © Fernand Hazan, Paris 1989
Copyright © ADAGP
English Translation Copyright © Bestseller Publications Ltd, 1989

All rights reserved. No part of this publication
may be reproduced, stored in a retrieval system,
or transmitted, in any form or by any means, electronic,
mechanical, photocopying, recording or otherwise,
without the prior permission of the copyright holder.

ISBN 1-85170-212-1

Printed and bound in Hong Kong

Matisse is the ideal trajectory: he begins with the painting of an old man and ends with the painting of a young one.

Pierre Alechinsky

Henri Matisse, who symbolizes, with Picasso, twentieth-century art at its most accomplished, was twenty years old when he chose to become a painter: there is no evidence of a precocious sense of 'vocation', nor of any frenzied curiosity about painting at an early age. In the early stages of his biography there is nothing to satisfy lovers of anecdote, nothing to confirm the romantic notion of the artist yoked to the wheel of destiny.

A BELATED INTRODUCTION TO PAINTING

Born on the last day of 1869 in his grandfather's house, in Cateau-Cambrésis, Henri Emile Benoît Matisse came from a '*petite bourgeoise*' family; his father ran, with the help of his wife, a small grain and hardware shop in Bohain-en-Vermandois (in the Saint-Quentin *arrondissement* where Matisse spent the whole of his childhood). There was nothing to indicate that the young Henri Matisse would eventually be seduced by the shelf labelled 'paints, colours and varnish' in his father's shop, nor can we confirm, as is maintained by certain biographers, that his mother indulged in plate decoration in her free moments (which must have been few and far between, snatched between taking care of the business and of her two children: a second son, Emile was born in 1872).

Matisse was later to describe his parents as 'simple people, but hard workers',[1] realizing that 'coming from a milieu that had no reason to push [him]' towards the fine arts, he should probably have 'succeeded [his] father as a grain merchant'.[2] Because of his delicate health, his parents decided that after studies in classics at the lycée Henri Martin, he would go on to take a law degree. Consequently, he received his diploma in Paris in August 1888, but during his stay in the capital, he evinced 'no desire to visit the great museums, or even the annual Salon de la Peinture' (see note 2).

In 1889, therefore, Matisse quite logically started work as a solicitor's clerk in Saint-Quentin. Did he nonetheless feel, to use the term Matisse himself employed to evoke this period, 'called' towards artistic pursuits? Each morning before work he attended classes in fabric embroidery in Saint-Quentin. Under the supervision of a former pupil of Bonnat, students would do applied drawing, obviously intended to supply the needs of the textile industry in the region. But during his stay in Saint-Quentin, Matisse made several visits to the Lecuyer museum, renowned for its collection of pastels by Fantin-Latour. Here he discovered the extreme subtleties of colour and, at the same time, the importance of the face. 'Moved by these fine faces, I then realized that each one was, in its own way, entirely personal. Leaving the museum, I was surprised by the variety of smiles, each particular to its own mask'.[3]

Nevertheless, it was not until the following year whilst he was convalescing from a complicated peritonitis operation, that the nature of his future life's work was revealed to him: his mother brought him a paint-box and some lithographs which he assiduously copied. This belated

1. *Message à sa Ville Natale*, drafted for the inauguration of the Matisse Museum in Cateau (1952); Fourcade, 320. *Ecrits et Propos sur l'Art* by Matisse was edited and carefully annotated by Dominique Fourcade (Hermann, Savoir collection, 1972). Quotations taken from this collection are simply indicated by the editor's name followed by the page number.
2. Fourcade, 319.
3. Fourcade, 176.

Matisse at the time of his marriage, 1898.

discovery of painting took the form of a conversion: from then on Matisse had 'the certitude of having found [his] right path'. In 1952 he was to say, 'I felt that I was in my own climate and not staring at a closed horizon as I had done in my previous life'. But the choice of a new career gave rise to some anxiety; everything about his new profession had to be learned from scratch: 'I threw myself head first into the work, motivated by the principle I had heard all my young life: "get a move on" . . . Like my parents I rushed into my work, urged on by I don't know what, by a force which I now realize was foreign to my life as a normal person' (see note 2). Perhaps we should interpret this 'get a move on', following the advice and the example of his parents, as the means by which Henri Matisse rediscovered a certain 'normality': in any case, the injunction can be seen at work in the frenzied manner in which he applied himself to his apprenticeship as a painter, once his father's suspicions about this unforeseen change of direction had been overcome – a step only achieved with the intervention of a former disciple of Bouguereau, whose name at the time was synonymous with the pinnacle of respectability and success (at least in the financial sense) in establishment painting.

THE APPRENTICESHIP YEARS

In October 1891, Henri Matisse accordingly entered the Julien Academy under William Bouguereau, the champion of the academic, antiseptic nude, whose pictorial theory was distilled as 'No ideas, especially no ideas!' The *maître* soon began to criticize Matisse for not drawing according to the rules; nevertheless, in 1892, he put him forward for admission to the Beaux-Arts – Matisse failed. Abandoning Bourguereau and the Julien Academy (deserted in the same period by Sérusier, after whose departure Bonnard, Vuillard and M. Denis followed suit) Matisse spent an equally short spell with another aca-

demic painter, Gabriel Ferrier. He enrolled at night-classes at the School of Decorative Arts in order to learn perspective. Here he met Marquet, six years his junior, and a long friendship between the two men began.

In the end it was in Gustave Moreau's studio that Matisse found the kind of teaching which suited him best. Making no attempt to influence his students or to convert them to his style, Moreau, the uncontested master of primitive symbolism, whose work belied the audacity of colour which few of his contemporaries appreciated, was much more concerned with initiating his students into the history of art than preparing them for the Salon.[4] His enthusiasm was all-embracing (he appreciated Lautrec as much as Veronese) and he encouraged his students to pay regular visits to the Louvre, to which admission was, at the time, free, encouraging them to copy the ancient masters. Matisse attended Moreau's workshops until his teacher's death.

During these years of apprenticeship, he developed an intense curiosity for all the models that painting could offer him. He made copies at the Louvre, where he discovered the range of the Dutch (see p.45), and acquired amongst his colleagues a reputation as a 'scholar of the art of the greys';[5] but his travels were to expose him to other influences. In 1895, with his neighbour from 19, Quai Saint-Michel, Emile Wéry, he worked on motif in Brittany. From that point on the Louvre was seen in contradistinction to the open air favoured by the

---

4. At the time, when the gallery circuit was still in its infancy and, the most important galleries were dealing almost exclusively in traditional painting, the Salon was the only route open to a painter looking for fame and, with it, the commissions that would enable him to earn a living from his art. But this also meant that the artist would have to concede to majority taste, as reflected by the jury, which consisted of academicians and official painters: Impressionism for example, was only sparsely represented.

5. With particular reference to *Bouquet de Fleurs* of 1894 (Cateau Museum), which has echos of the Dutch painters: the canvas is in a classical style, but in the background a framed painting and a mirror introduce the question, later to become a Matisse characteristic, of the painting within the painting, opening up the space of representation with the reflection of light in the mirror.

The Serf, *bronze, 1900–1903, height 92 cm.*

Impressionists, and Matisse's palette began tentatively to brighten, even if he still adhered to the conventional rules of composition. Also in 1895, he discovered the works of Cézanne at the house of the art dealer, Vollard. He was particularly struck by Cézanne's ambition to create works which would rival those in the great museums but which obeyed other principles. A second spell in Brittany the following summer (during which he visited Belle-Ile, la Pointe du Raz and Pont-Aven, though he remained unaware of Gauguin whose work he did not fully appreciate at that point) brought a meeting with the Australian painter, John Peter Russell, who was very open to Impressionism. Russell gave him two Van Gogh drawings and arranged a meeting with Rodin (in fact the meeting was not a great success, even though Matisse took notice of the drawings pinned to the sculptor's wall, which he would remember when he himself came to work with volume) and another with Pissarro, who informed him, most notably, that, 'an impressionist is a painter who never duplicates the same painting . . . Cézanne is not an impressionist. He is a classicist because [whether he was painting] bathers, Mont-Sainte-Victoire or other subjects, he painted the same painting all his life'.[6]

1896 also saw Matisse's participation in his first Salon de la Société Nationale des Beaux Arts (in the Champs de Mars). There he presented four canvases, one of which, *The Reader* was acquired by the state for the Château de Rambouillet.[7] This first success was confirmed by his election as associate member of the Salon. The following year (during which he was able to study the Impressionists at closer range thanks to the Caillebotte bequest to the Luxembourg museum), he exhibited two interiors and three still lifes, whose treatment and sombre tonalities now appear cautious: with some justification, however, *The Dining Table* was accepted.

---

6. Fourcade, 44.
7. When Matisse wanted to show *La Liseuse* at the 1900 Exhibition, the jury rejected it.

TURNER AND THE 'MIDI'

In 1898, Matisse acknowledged his daughter Marguerite, who had been born four years earlier, and married Amélie Parayre, originally from Toulouse. The young couple left for London on honeymoon, but also 'specially to see the Turners' (on Pissarro's advice) which Matisse placed as 'the passage between tradition and Impressionism'.[8] The question of this 'passage' (between the Louvre and the open air) preoccupied him a great deal, and gave him increasing cause for thought after the spring of 1898 when he travelled to Corsica (where his sister-in-law lived), and to Toulouse (staying with his parents-in-law) and was overcome by the violent splendour of natural light, fascinated, as a 'man from the north', with the special qualities of the Mediterranean: 'it was in Ajaccio that I first began to marvel at the south'.[9] The small paintings produced in Corsica and in the weeks that followed bear witness to this 'wonder' with a violent rush of bright colour, not always under control, but constantly asserting, in its enthusiasm and its generosity of touch, the wish to break with the 'art of the grey' in order to achieve a new conception of light and of the relationship between colour and drawing, with the help of the open air.

Having sent four of these 'pocket-sketches' to Henri Evenpoël, his closest friend from his studio days, he received a somewhat alarmed reply, reproaching him not only for the new violence in his painting, but also for not completing the work: 'it is the *painting of exasperation . . .* that is all the development you have achieved! . . . why be satisfied with such summary and approximate impressions?'[10] (Evenpoël, who described himself as 'Moreau's stick-in-the-mud student', may have been recalling the master's comment to Matisse: 'You are going to simplify painting' . . . but the accusation of leaving his work 'unfinished' was frequently levelled at Matisse.) The painter himself qualified this submission to the power of colour as 'exasperation': Turner was a long way off, as was the transition from tradition to Impressionism; Matisse was in fact exceeding the boundaries of everything that had been allowed hitherto. By stretching tones to the peak of their intensity, he relaxed the constraints on colour and achieved an emancipation of colour itself, independent of the motif it defines. At this point in his work we find paradoxical treatments of planes, in which the motif, from a traditional point of view, is poorly conceived. It was, however, a decisive experience from which Matisse was to draw important long-term lessons.

CEZANNE AND SCULPTURE

Matisse returned to Paris in 1899. Gustave Moreau was dead, and his studio had been taken over by Cormon, a specialist in pre-historic scenes, who swiftly eased Matisse out on the grounds that, at thirty, he was too old to be a student.[11] He enrolled at the Camillo Academy where Carrière was teaching and where he met Derain, Jean Puy, Chabaud and Laprade. Carrière never 'corrected' Matisse's work: 'he told me, some years later, that he wished to respect my idea, and this is what interested him'.[12] This 'idea' was the synthesis he sought between the memory of Mediterranean colour and light and the rigorousness of construction inspired by Cézanne. As

---

8. Fourcade, 124.
9. Fourcade, 104.
10. Letter of the 6th June, 1898, published in the Henri Matisse Notebooks, no. 4.

---

11. In its fourth issue (May 15th), the dealer Paul Guillaume's review *Les Arts à Paris* published the following commentary opposite a full-page photo of *The Serf*: 'M. Cormon, painter, member of the Institute, is founding a society "Le Club Artistique de France", whose aim is to strive against the tendencies of the modern school of painting, sculpture and music. Are you afraid, M. Cormon? Do you have so little confidence in your own talent that you have to struggle against modernism?'
12. R. Escholier, *Matisse, Ce Vivant*, Fayard, 1956, p.43.

Matisse sculpting.

Matisse saw it, Cézanne was becoming more and more influential: to the extent that he actually bought *Three Bathers* from Vollard (along with a Van Gogh, a plaster bust by Rodin and a small Gauguin), a purchase which obliged him to sell his wedding-ring; the Matisse household, with two sons, Jean, born in 1899 and Pierre, in 1900, was not prospering. From then on Matisse refused to be separated from the *Bathers*. Until he finally donated it to the museum of the Petit Palais, he continued to find in the picture the comfort and encouragement he needed in moments of uncertainty. More subtle was the influence of the painting's mythological aspect. References to the Golden Age are to be found in Matisse's own work up until 1910–11. 'If Cézanne is right, I am right', 'Cézanne is the master of us all': these were just some of Matisse's expressions of admiration for Cézanne – even if he was to add 'colour, this magic, even after him . . . is yet to be found'.[13]

More urgently, Matisse's father had stopped his allowance as a protest against his quitting the Beaux Arts. It is true that he had sold a few works (the most impersonal) to the state, but he was nonetheless obliged, while his wife worked as a milliner, to join Marquet in the decoration of the Grand Palais for the Universal Exhibition of 1900. This involved the painting of mile upon mile of garlands but, even so, he still found time to go to life-form classes in the rue Etienne Marcel. For two years he worked on an interpretation of Barye's *Jaguar Devouring a Hare*, studying its anatomy and movement with passion ('first with the eyes . . . then with eyes closed, with notions of volume that only the touch can give'). To pursue his anatomical studies further he acquired a dissected cat from an assistant at the Beaux Arts in order to analyse the back and the paws.[14] In the winter of 1900, he began work on *The Serf*, a male study of rare power: its rugged surface suggests a

dynamism which the static body would lack if treated more calmly. From now on, sculpture would act as a kind of resting-post between paintings: 'As the research is the same, if I get tired of one medium, then I turn to the other . . . To express form, I sometimes give myself over to sculpture, which allows me, instead of being fixed before a flat surface, to move around the object in order to understand it better'.[15] Pierre Schneider has pointed out that 'Matisse applied himself more particularly to sculpture between 1900 and 1910 and 1925 and 1930, specifically in periods when his painting tended towards the two-dimensional. He used sculpture to counterbalance this tendency, to affirm a sense of volumes and masses'.[16] As for the complementary nature of the two approaches, this is graphically and symbolically revealed in the frequent representation of Matisse's sculptures (bearing the same titles as the canvases) in his painting.

His fervent attitude to the work-process which he frequently pursued in contradictory directions (during this period he continued to make copies at the Louvre) finally came to light in a series of exhibitions which were to bring some recognition for the Matisse signature (although his financial situation remained precarious – the family was obliged to return to Bohain for a while, where Matisse's father remained sceptical about his son painting). In 1901, Matisse took part in the first Salon des Indépendants presided over by Paul Signac, and in 1902, thanks to Roger Marx, he participated in an exhibition of former students of Moreau which brought about his first gallery sale.[17] In 1903, he once again exhibited at the

13. Fourcade, 14.
14. Aragon, *Matisse-en-France*. (1942), *Henri Matisse, Roman*, Gallimard, 1971, vol. I, p.81.

15. Fourcade, 70.
16. Catalogue of the Centenary Exhibition, Grand Palais, Paris, p.23.
17. A former antique dealer, Berthe Weil ran one of the few galleries exhibiting 'advanced' painting. It was the first to exhibit Matisse, but also Vlaminck, Marquet, Modigliani, Van Dongen, Dufy, Metzinger, etc. Legend has it that she maintained a ceiling on prices of 100 francs 'whatever the importance of the work submitted by the artist. Her excuse was that she sold virtually nothing' (J.-P. Crespelle. *Vlaminck, Fauve de la Peinture*, Gallimard, 1958, p.110): in fact, it seems that Matisse's painting was sold for 130 francs (of which the painter received 110 francs).

Matisse and the Serpentine, *Matisse sculpting, 1913.*
Musée d'Orsay, Paris.

Indépendants, but also at the first Autumn Salon, which was also showing a posthumous retrospective of Gauguin (about whom Matisse was beginning to have a change of opinion). This was the year in which he took up engraving, notably etchings and dry-point.

Just after his first one-man exhibition at the Vollard gallery (forty-five canvases and a drawing, spanning 1897 to 1903), he was invited by Signac to spend the summer at his villa in Saint-Tropez. On his return to Paris in the autumn, the Beaux Arts bought his copy of *Balthazar Castiglione* by Raphael. Matisse began work on *Luxe, calme et volupté* doing his best faithfully to apply divisionist theories. When it was exhibited at the Indépendants the following year, it was immediately purchased by Signac himself (see p.52).

At the Autumn Salon of 1905, which featured a homage to Cézanne (about thirty works in all), Matisse exhibited thirteen canvases. Over these few years, it appeared that various inclinations (the Louvre and research, personal work and exterior theory, Cézanne and Post-Impressionism) were coming together and demanding that a choice be made.

1905: THE '*CAGE AUX FAUVES*'

Matisse made this 'choice', or rather this leap forward, in Collioure during the summer of 1905. He had postponed making it since 1898 because of the constant need to know more, and to put certain 'solutions' to the test personally in order to prove that they were, for him, dead ends. Matisse had meetings with Maillol in Banyuls (finding himself in tacit disagreement with the latter's conception of sculpture), and more particularly, with Daniel de Monfried. Monfried showed Matisse his Gauguins, demonstrating the qualities inherent in these works which had been a formative influence on his own painting since 1890 (luminous colours and the organiza-

tion of background into contrasting wedges of colour), but in which Matisse found only confirmation of the sterility of Divisionism. There is an important commentary on Matisse's personal research to be found in the letters Derain wrote to Vlaminck at this time: 'he has shown me photographs of his canvases; they are quite extraordinary. I think he has stepped through the door into the seventh garden, the garden of happiness. He is going through a crisis at the moment as far as painting is concerned. But, on the other hand, he is a much more extraordinary character than I would ever have imagined in terms of his logic and his psychological speculations'.[18] The 'crisis' Derain refers to is certainly the necessity Matisse felt to abandon all supports, all existing models (including the *avant-garde*) in order to pursue solely what he called his 'feeling', his 'emotion', the relationship between painter and model reconstructed exclusively by pictorial means. Matisse was convinced that there was a 'logic' to be found which could apply to this process of reconstructing 'feeling', having recently experimented with the pictorial logic of others (Cézanne, Post-Impressionism, Divisionism). The product of this logic was *Woman with Hat*, (p.55), *The Green Ray* (both portraits of Madame Matisse), and *Portrait of Derain*, three canvases painted in Collioure which Matisse saw as the logical consequence of his decision-making, but which were to play their part, at the Autumn Salon, in the 'Fauvism' scandal.

Hung together in room 7 the contributions of Matisse, Derain, O. Friesz, Manguin, Puy, Rouault, Valtat and Vlaminck appeared to public and critics alike as the deliberate expression of a joint aggressive will, and this impression was enhanced by the very proximity of the paintings one to another. The boldness of colour, the schematism of what is, effectively, drawing (even if it is always the drawing which provides the accessibility of a

18. Derain, *Lettres à Vlaminck*, Flammarion, 1955, pp.149 and 161.

work from the point of view of academic ability) seemed unacceptable. *L'Illustration* of 1st November published a collection of reproductions with commentaries by Gustave Geffroy and Louis Vauxcelles (who coined the term 'Fauves', but nonetheless estimated that 'M. Matisse is one of the most strongly gifted of today's painters'). Here we find the assertion that Matisse 'has strayed with the others into eccentricities of colour from which he will no doubt return of his own accord', and that 'concern for colour suffers in the passionate research into which he is prepared to immerse himself'.[19] Disappointed with this response, Matisse, who was in no way looking for scandal, wrote to Signac: 'For the first time in my life I was happy to exhibit, because my pieces are unimportant perhaps, but they have the merit of expressing my sensations in a very pure way'.[20] Doubtless it was precisely this 'purity', this absence of 'civility' ('fauve' means wild) which shocked. Perhaps to understand the violence of contemporary reaction, we should recall the way in which apartments of the period were furnished – after all a painting was also created to be hung on a wall and the canvases Matisse presented to the notorious '*Cage aux Fauves*' are certainly in a format designed to be hung. It is clear that this type of painting is thoroughly incompatible with the over-abundance of furniture, ornaments and wall-hangings which characterized the suffocating internal decor at the end of the nineteenth century; but it is equally incompatible with the 'modern style' with its floral volutes and decorative arabesques which was favoured by what was still a small number of 'advanced' spirits. In such a context, an Impressionist painting – in so far as the public had begun to be able to discern what that meant – would certainly be incongruous, but because it was a gentle and euphoric piece of escapism. *The Green Ray* or *Window at Collioure*, on the

other hand, would have produced an irreversible disharmony, the assertion of a frank and offensive opposition. Thirty years later, Matisse was to explain to Tériade that this was the departure point for Fauvism, 'the beautiful reds, beautiful blues, beautiful yellows, materials which shake the sensual roots of men'.[21] This shaking of the sensual roots was an effort to redirect painting towards a relationship more fundamentally concerned with feelings and senses than anything hither to attempted, including Impressionism. For the Impressionists sensibility was confined to the visual, remaining synonymous with fleeting sensation; whereas Matissian 'sensuality' is at once more synthetic and more durable, being achieved by increasing insistence upon motif.

It is not difficult to imagine the effect Matisse's radical 'leap forward' must have had on his contemporaries – Marcel Duchamp, for instance, although Matisse's influence is barely discernible in his work[22] – making him the quasi-official 'leader' of Fauvism, even though he considered its appearance as a 'school' to be due to the more or less gratuitous presentation of the 1905 exhibition. The painters grouped together on that occasion had already exhibited individually without causing such an outcry and 'later, each one disowned, according to his personality, that part of fauvism which he found excessive in order to follow his own path'.[23] As far as Matisse was concerned, and as the evolution of his work was to show, he refused to allow himself to be fettered by any so-called 'Fauvist' theory and he only retained from this period[24]

19. This page was ironically reproduced in January 1929, in *Les Arts de Paris*.
20. Letter of 29th September 1915, cited by P. Schneider, *Matisse*, Flammarion, 1984, p.222.

21. Fourcade, 128.
22. 'It was at the Autumn Salon of 1905 that the idea of painting came to me . . . Oh! it was Matisse obviously. Yes, he was at the beginning of it all . . . his paintings at the Autumn Salon move me a lot; it was a big affair at the time, you know. It had a lot of impact' (*Entretiens avec Pierre Cabanne*, Belfond, 1967, pp.32–33.
23. Fourcade, 117.
24. Although certain commentators saw the way Matisse's art developed as covering the full range of possibilities suggested by Fauvism, describing the author of *The Green Ray* as '*le fauve par excellence*', many others reproached him for renouncing the most audacious and 'anarchistic' aspects of his

that which assisted the progress of the practical application of his painting. Everything that was to distinguish him from the other 'fauves' manifested itself very quickly: while the others submitted to the immediate expressive power of colour (which was also to be a characteristic of the German Expressionists), Matisse studied colour in terms of the relationships it generates. He knew perfectly well that the canvas is constructed not by the isolated surface, but by a totality of colour-agreements: if red and green have been placed together in a harmonic relationship, the introduction of a blue will disturb this harmony and necessitate a rebalancing of colour which, as the painting progresses, takes over the whole of the surface – affecting both forms and their importance. Viewed in this way, colour can appear totally independent of all concern for a realistic representation of the original subject: this was precisely the process which confirmed the painting's autonomy, its 'pure' existence, liberated from that which served originally as pretext.

THE BENEFICIAL EFFECTS OF SCANDAL

Matisse was surprised and disappointed by the scandal of 1905: certain back-biters alleged that he dared not enter the 'Cage aux Fauves' such was the public vitriol which greeted his *Woman with Hat*. However, this was the work bought by Michael and Sarah Stein. Léo Stein condemned it as an 'ugly daub', but wanted to keep it, precisely to be able to understand its fascination. This introduction into the circle of Gertrude Stein, whose apartment on the rue de Fleurus was a regular meeting-place for progressive artists and intellectuals, was part of

a growing reputation from which Matisse continued to benefit right up to the beginning of the first world war, by which time he had become the most important painter of the Paris School.

In 1906, the Druet gallery organized a one-man exhibition (fifty-five works) which was fairly successful. That year he showed only one painting at the Salon des Indépendants: *La Joie de vivre* (see p.61), which caused a scandal once again, but was immediately acquired by Léo Stein (it is probable that Picasso's *Demoiselles d'Avignon* was conceived the following winter as a kind of reply to *Joie de vivre*). Matisse then took off on a two-week trip to Algeria where he responded with indifference if not hostility to all manner of exoticism ('the famous Ouled-Nails, what a joke! We have seen a hundred times better at the Exhibition',[25] and all he brought back was a small pottery vase. He was delighted to be back in Collioure where he spent the rest of the summer. Here he painted *Blue Nude (Souvenir de Biskra)* (see p.63) which he was to exhibit the following year at the Salon des Indépendants. In Gertrude Stein's apartment, he was introduced to Picasso. It is difficult to imagine two more opposite characters. While Matisse would gladly hold forth on the subject of painting, Picasso, twelve years his junior, although his artistic career had begun earlier, was more taciturn. Contemporary observers noted that the elegance of the one contrasted with the dandyish bohemianism of the other.[26] Even though Matisse had few real friends, being surrounded by a 'gang' like the one in the

---

painting. Significantly, an exhibition in 1966 presenting 'French Fauvism and the beginnings of German Expression', selected Matisse paintings from the period between 1896 and 1909.

25. Letter to Manguin, cited by P. Schneider, op. cit. p.158.
26. Fernande Olivier, Picasso's companion, described Matisse thus: 'A kind of grand master; regular features, fine golden beard . . . a sympathetic demeanour. He seems to be retreating behind his large spectacles, but he comes to life as soon as painting is mentioned. Then he will start to discuss, assert and want to convince' (*Picasso and his Friends*, Stock, 1933, p.37). A rather more ambiguous appreciation came from Salmon: 'An occasional guest at Picasso's studio, Henri Matisse, the bearded painter with the gold-rimmed glasses, brought a severe tone into the discussion, a tone of "professional gravity" . . . not in the nature of our circle . . . he was suspicious of us.'

rue Ravignan was not to his taste. Nevertheless there was a profound sympathy between the two painters; each was aware of the other's value and recognized the other as his own most serious rival: 'Matisse knew that Picasso was Picasso just as Picasso knew that Matisse was Matisse' (Jean Cassou[27]). Temporary disappointments and tensions apart (notably when Cubism became the dominant element in the *avant-garde* and the '*bande de Picasso*', from Salmon to Cocteau, thought fit to attack Matisse) the relationship between the two painters recalls what Nietzsche, describing great thoughts which communicate with each other throughout history despite their apparent differences, had called a *stellar friendship*.

In 1907 Matisse went to Italy for the first time. He developed a great passion for the primitives, but was less enthusiastic about the Renaissance of Michelangelo and Leonardo da Vinci which he considered 'decadent'. He made another trip to Collioure, and exhibited his first version of *Luxe* (see p.67) at the Autumn Salon. Towards the end of the year, Apollinaire, who preferrred compositions like *Joie de vivre* and *Luxe* to pure Fauvism, devoted an article-interview to Matisse in *La Phalange*. As he saw it, Matisse's 'reasonable' art combined 'the most tender qualities of France: its simple strength and gentle clarity'. This comment established an insistence on the 'national' character of Matisse's painting, which was later to resurface with Aragon.

At the instigation of Sarah Stein and Hans Purrmann, Matisse opened an 'Academy' in 1908, first in the rue de Sèvres and then in the Boulevard des Invalides, to which many young artists flocked, particularly the Germans ('the Matisse Academy, the biggest of the fauvist schools, was the cradle of the cosmopolitan Ecole de Paris', Salmon wrote). But two years later he abandoned the

Reclining Figure, Head in Hand, *1929, engraving.
Print Department, Bibliothèque Nationale, Paris.*

project, complaining that it took up too much of his time to the detriment of his own work: 'I refused to accept remuneration for my criticisms, not wishing to be financially involved should ever I wish to leave'.[28] Nonetheless this experience confirms the 'pedagogical' side to Matisse's genius, in which the serious and the liberal cohabit as we can observe in the notes taken by Sarah Stein, and which is ingrained in his constant desire to explain the intentions behind his painting. His texts and interviews reveal that, for Matisse, it was not a question of theory, *a priori*, but of drawing lessons from each successive step forward in his work. Theory exists first and foremost *in* the painting which, at the moment of realization, is always in advance of 'ideas'. This is the theme of *Notes d'un Peintre*, published by *La Grande Revue* in the December issue of 1908. Rapidly translated into German and Russian, it was to reinforce his international reputation (in 1908 two exhibitions were held, one in New York at the Stieglitz gallery, the other in Berlin for Cassirer, though this latter was something of a flop).

27. Interview with Laurence Bertrand Dorleac, in *Histoire de l'Art. Paris 1940–1944*, Sorbonne Publications, 1987, p.310. cf. Picasso himself, cited by M. Pleynet (*Tel Quel* no 37): 'No-one has ever looked at Matisse's painting as closely as I have. And he at mine.'

28. Matisse, in Escholier, op. cit., p.79.

AN 'ART OF BALANCE'

Notes d'un Peintre puts forward formulae which were often badly received. Here we find the famous declaration: 'What I dream of is an art of balance, of purity, of tranquillity, devoid of disturbing or disquieting subject-matter, which will be for everyone who works with the mind, a businessman or a man of letters for example, a balm, a soothing influence on the mind, something like a good armchair that provides relief from bodily fatigue'[29] – a credo that Matisse upheld until the end of his career, declaring to Georges Charbonnier for example: 'my role is to soothe'[29] and, in 1954, that he chose 'to put torment and anxiety behind him', committing himself to the transcription of the beauty of the world and to the joy of painting.[30] It has been said that this also betrays a sobering or a toning down of his painting, that from this point on his work is characterized by a facile and superficial charm, that it is merely entertaining and lacking in depth (the later *Odalisques* could, on first sight, be interpreted in this way). However, that particular interpretation is contradicted by the canvases Matisse painted in the next few years – amongst which we find some of the greatest works of the century (*The Dance*, 1909; *The Red Studio* and *Interior with Aubergines*, 1911; *Portrait of Madame Matisse*, 1912–13; *The French Window in Collioure*, 1914, and so on; pp.73–97). It is also at odds with other passages from *Notes d'un Peintre* where the visionary nature of painting is vigorously stressed: beneath the changing appearances of things, 'we can devine a nature which is more real, more essential, to which the artist fixes himself in order to give a more durable interpretation of reality'.[31] Here Matisse is obviously distancing himself from Impressionism (and also from the deliquescent character of painting in the modern style); but, in 1908, he also insisted on the division which separated him from Cubism which was beginning to gain notoriety: 'people who obstinately adhere to style, deliberately divorcing themselves from nature do not arrive at the truth'.[32] 'The art of balance . . . something like a good armchair' should therefore be understood as the antithesis to the '*style de parti pris*': the formula is not perhaps entirely successful (taken out of context, it would seem to advocate a kind of painting which is, in fact, unacceptable), but it does represent an expression of the highest ambition – to turn painting into a transposition of the emotional presence of things, a way of access to the truth of the world which inspires our 'sensuality'.

These *Notes d'un Peintre* are prefaced in *La Grande Revue* by a short text by Georges Desvallières, justifying its inclusion by the controversy Matisse's work provoked ('contempt, anger or admiration'). It is true that at this time Matisse still had few supporters in France – with the exception of people like Marcel Sembat or André Level who, between 1904 and 1914, acquired ten canvases for the collectors' association *La Peau de l'Ours*, and later, Jacques Doucet, who only bought *Goldfish and Palette* (p.99) on the insistence of his advisors Louis Aragon and André Breton.[33] On the other hand, Matisse did enjoy the support of the Steins and a few American collectors, along with Shchukin whom he met at Gertrude Stein's apartment in 1906. Shchukin bought several paintings

---

29. Fourcade, 50. Léger declared later: 'we must distract the man from his enormous and often disagreeable effort, envelop him, make him live in a new and preponderant plastic order', attributing to his own work the role of 'sedative', not provoking the least reaction – but he had the reputation of being a painter who cared about the 'people' and the subjects he treats appear, unlike those of Matisse, to be imbued with 'social' preoccupations.
30. Fourcade, 51.
31. Fourcade, 45.

32. Fourcade, 52. Matisse always criticized intellectualism, which he saw as a danger to painting: 'for me, it is the sensation which comes first, then the idea. I see a bouquet of flowers, it pleases me, I do something. If the Cubists conceive an idea, and they then ask: "what sensation does it give me?" – well, I quite simply do not understand this process' (1949, Fourcade, 96 to 97). In 1919, André Lhote remarked that 'whereas Matisse proceeds from sensation to idea, the cubists proceed from idea to sensation'.
33. The same resistance in Belgium: writing about the Autumn Salon of 1913, in *L'Art Moderne*, G. Jean-Aubry said: 'but about Matisse, I will say nothing, where is this leading? Where does it come from? No-one knows'.

including *The Red Dining Table* (p.69), and he commissioned *Music* and *The Dance* to decorate his vast house in Moscow. Ivan Morosov, who came with Shchukin to the workshop in 1908 and whose tastes were initially more traditional than his fellow Russian,[34] was the most important buyer of the 'Moroccan' paintings (exhibited in 1913 at the Bernheim-Jeune gallery). Sales and commissions, therefore, brought a certain amount of financial security, and this was confirmed in 1909, when Matisse signed a contract with the Bernheim-Jeune gallery, to which he had been introduced by the critic Felix Fénéon. It is noteworthy that the price negotiated in this first contract (for his entire output), was significantly higher than that which Derain obtained, for example, three years later from Kahnweiler: Matisse was paid 1,875 francs for a half-length format (116 × 89cm), Derain received only 500 francs. These prices remained unchanged for Matisse when the contract was renewed in 1912, but the third contract, of 19th October, 1917, represented a significant rise: 4,500 francs for a half-length; rising even higher in 1920 (7,000 francs) and again in 1912 (11,000 francs) even though, since 1917, Matisse had been obliged to deliver only half of his output.[35] No doubt the general rise in the cost of living partially explains these periodic re-evaluations,[36] but it seems clear that by now Matisse represented a gilt-edged investment for dealers and collectors. On 2nd March, 1914, the sale at the Hôtel Drouot, of works assembled by *La Peau de l'Ours*, provided further confirmation that painting by living artists could be a sound investment (something that had not always been the case). The ten Matisse canvases in

the sale ranged from 600 (*Effet de Neige*, 27 × 34cm) to 5,000 francs (*Compotier de Pommes et Oranges*, 46 × 56cm). The latter exceeded – in many cases by quite a lot – the prices obtained by the other artists on show (which included such highly regarded figures as Bonnard, M. Denis, Derain, Marquet, Dufy, Maillol, Sérusier) with the exception of Picasso, who obtained 11,500 and 5,200 francs, respectively, for *Les Bateleurs* (canvas, 225 × 235cm), and *Les Trois Hollandaises* (gouache on card, 77 × 67cm) though these were much larger works. Matisse was certainly the most expensive artist, with a value of between 60 and 500 francs a point, as against 45 to 400 francs a point for Picasso.

TRAVELLING, MOROCCO

Assured from now on of a regular income, Matisse rented a house at Issy-les-Moulineaux after receiving a commission from Shchukin (he needed a large studio properly to realize the work). 'Ten minutes ride (54 trains a day) from Montparnasse': a square, two-storey building, surrounded by a huge garden with two ponds. It had a bathroom and a greenhouse, both equally appreciated by the family, and the bois de Clamart nearby for horseback riding. Three years later, Matisse bought the house, and worked there regularly between his increasingly frequent trips abroad.

Between 1910 and 1914, he went to Munich, where he visited with Marquet an exhibition of Islamic art which confirmed his taste for certain aspects of the Orient he had first discovered in 1903 at the museum of Decorative Arts and documented with photographs. He also travelled to Spain (mid-November 1910 to January 1911); to Moscow (1911, to supervise the hanging of his canvases in Shchukin's house, but discovering while he was there the richness of colour in Byzantine icons: another aspect of the Orient); to Morocco (in 1911 and 1912). In 1914,

---

34. But he is obviously not alone: in his article on the Autumn Salon of 1912 for the Russian review *Apollo*, Tugendhold recognized that Matisse certainly had talent, but qualified him as a perpetrator of gaudy wall-posters.
35. See Raymonde Moulin: *Le Marché de la Peinture en France*, Minuit, 1967, p.544.
36. 'Modern painting. Artists want to be paid more. We learn from the newspapers that parts for motor-cars have incrfeased in pricce by 88 per cent. Matisse by 75, Georges Bernheim'. R. Gimpel, *Journal d'un Collectionneur Marchand de Tableaux*, Calmann-Levy, 1963, p.169.

when he was not drafted (Marcel Sembat, Minister for War, apparently gave this reply to Matisse and Marquet, who were anxious to know how to best serve their country: 'by continuing just as you are, by painting well'), . he returned to Collioure with Marquet, and, significantly, made the acquaintance of Juan Gris.

What did he retain from these trips? Still very little of the exotic (on each homecoming he declared himself happy to be back 'in his slippers'), but rather the confirmation of his interests: for a certain light (which in Tangier was 'so soft, quite different to the Mediterranean'[37]) and the arrangement of decorative arabesques or the luxuriance of printed fabrics (two canvases, painted in Seville, *Still life – Spain* and *Still life – Seville* take their motif from locally bought shawls). More specifically, Morocco allowed him to re-establish his contact with nature, and to rid himself of the vestiges of a Fauvist approach which had become stifling.

This is evident in the still lifes painted in Tangier in 1913. The space around the motif had become more complex whether it consisted of an orange bowl (see p.91) or of *Arums, Irises and Mimosas* (Pushkin Museum), which was one of his first still lifes in large format (140 × 87cm). In these two paintings, the fabric decoration is directly integrated into the construction of patterns, the colours are extremely gentle, and the falling view-point gives an allusive perspective. In Tangier, Matisse encountered the kind of nature and models which radiated a certain *joie de vivre*: he nevertheless resisted the temptation of a third trip, perhaps fearing a dilution of his work, the fading of his colours into a decidedly dangerous gentility.

But the two trips he did make provided him with the opportunity to conceive, with the *Moroccan Triptych* (Pushkin Museum) a kind of pictorial space offering a new solution to the problem inherent in the Shchukin commission (initially three large canvases, though the last one, *Bathers by a River* (see p.107) was not finished until 1916) which was not to be fully realized until he completed his work at the chapel in Vence. This difficulty lay in how to express a sense of completeness in a series of works, to transcend the unity of the single canvas without resorting to simple narrative? For such a project, he had to generalize the pictorial space (in 1916, Matisse was to read *La Science et l'Hypothèse* by Poincaré, in which he discovered an analysis of non-euclidian space in geometry).

The left-hand part of the triptych (*Window at Tangier*) was painted during the first trip to Morocco, before March 1912, and may have been conceived initially as an independent work, the idea of unifying it with the two other panels only emerging as he worked on these later sections in the autumn of 1912, during his second visit to North Africa. In a letter to Morosov in April 1913, Matisse specified that the three canvases should be hung together, and even provided an explanatory schema. Such an arrangement juxtaposes three paintings whose subject matter has little in common. On the left there is an urban landscape viewed from a hotel window; in the middle (*Zorah on the Terrace*) a female figure kneeling on a plain carpet, between a pair of Turkish slippers and a goldfish bowl; on the right, (*Entrance to the Casbah*) another urban landscape, perceived through an opening, but whose formal outlines are very different to those of its counterpart. Both view-point and scale change from one panel to another. But the three canvases possess an incontestable unity, which is entirely due to the light, to a bluish colouring which, in its subtle variations envelops the figure, the objects and architecture in a halo of gentle calm. Although each part of the triptych is boldly geometric in its construction, their juxtaposition makes the lines of construction imperceptible and generates an impression of perfect ease in the observer. This dialectic is as valid for the motifs as it is for the pictorial technique.

---

37. Letter to Camoin, 1st March, 1912, Fourcade, 117.

Matisse and his model Michaella at Vence, 1946.

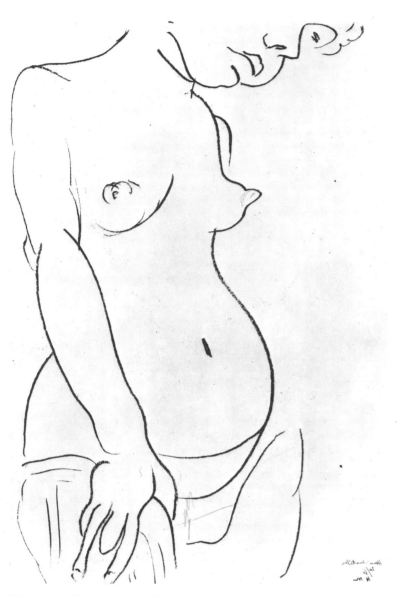

Nude with Cut face, *1914, lithograph.*
Print Department, Bibliothèque Nationale, Paris.

Subjects which, considered in isolation, could be simply a *souvenir du Maroc* (and thereby reduce 'pure painting' to 'exotic painting' in a kind of modernized oriental tradition) are transformed into what Matisse called 'emotion', indicated here by three heterogeneous angles on one 'place' united by a single light. Zorah, the view from the window and the casbah entrance suggest very much a single emotion produced by the town. They are the

interchangeable signs of this emotion in that their visual alignment persuades the eye to move from one to the other. But there is nothing anecdotal or sentimentally banal about the unifying factor. What they have in common is their basis, their foundation in what we might well call 'the essence' of the town – not in any idealist or platonic sense, but more as a sensual representation (like a smell) or a material transcription of how it feels to be there immersed in its light and colours, its shapes and lines.

While Matisse was travelling, there were increasing numbers of exhibitions of his work in other countries; in London and New York in 1910 and 1911; and in 1913 at the Armory Show, which brought modern art in all its diversity to the United States. Here Matisse was represented by one sculpture, three drawings and thirteen canvases, amongst which *Blue Nude* was sufficiently shocking to be burned in effigy in the streets. In 1913 his work was included at the Sezession in Berlin. While in France he continued to exhibit at various Salons and, on a regular basis, at the Berheim-Jeune gallery. Pictorial research was accompanied by intense work on sculpture: *La Serpentine, Back* I and II. Between 1910 and 1913 he worked on the five busts of Jeanette. From an initial cast still faithful to the model, they went through progressive modifications in bronze with variations to the hair style, the length of the neck, the inscription of the eye-sockets, all representing Matisse's efforts to achieve the same state of visual autonomy as in painting. To this end, he took on another studio in Paris (quai Saint-Michel) where he devoted all his energies, alternately, to his two modes of expression.

He still worked at Issy (particularly in the summer) during the early years of the war – exploring those elements of Cubism which he considered compatible with his own art (he actually retained only certain superficial characteristics, for example in *Pink and White Head*, 1914); the crystallization of his impressions of Tangier

(*The Moroccans*, 1916, p.105) and the organization of paintings based on the intimacy of family life (*The Piano Lessons*, 1916, p.103). In fact, his mastery was such that he could permit himself to come and go between works of research and other more 'classical' pieces: two versions of the same theme (*The Piano Lesson* and *The Music Lesson*) are not uncommon; and, in 1917, he produced the third manifestation of the relief *Back II*. It is also possible that working with a new model (Laurette) for a few years from the end of 1915, encouraged this development of variations on a theme. We know that Matisse always maintained a demanding relationship with his models, affectionate, but a little tyrannical at the same time – as if he was afraid of not being able to draw the maximum out of himself. What the artist himself said in 1954, speaking about the portrait, was that 'it demanded of the artist very particular gifts and the possibility of an almost complete identification of the painter with his model'.[38] This point can be generalized: the model is there to elicit 'identification' (it is often pointed out that Matisse worked physically in close contact with his model) and not to be faithfully represented; that is to say, the model must firstly give rise to an emotion capable of engendering a desire for identification, and only after many sessions can this emotion be translated into pictorial terms.

Even though Matisse completed several of his major works during the war years, we should not conclude that he was indifferent to events. In fact, 'behind us, things are not at all amusing', he wrote in a letter to Derain in 1916.[39] 'Add to our beautiful, eternally fleeting, painter's *métier* – beautiful only in dreams – the lack of news of my family and the anxiety which comes from the continuous waiting in which we live, the little we know, all that is hidden from us, and you have the image of the civilian in war time' – a civilian who, moreover, was extremely concerned about the fate of his painter friends and who, speaking of his work to his correspondent, Hans Purrmann, added, 'these are the important things in my life. I cannot say that it is not a struggle – but the real struggle is not there, I know perfectly well, and it is with marked respect that I think about the *poilus* who modestly say: "we are forced to be here". This war will have positive results – what gravity will it have given to the lives of even those who did not take part in it if they can share the feelings of the simple soldier'.[40]

THE FIRST NICE PERIOD

In 1916, Matisse stayed in Nice for the first time. Here he discovered a climate and a light which completely seduced him, and after 1920 he spent half the year there (the other half in Paris) in an apartment in the Place Charles Félix. Later, in 1938, he was to take up residence in the Regina, on the Colline de Cimiez which dominates the town. But light is not simply the same thing as lighting, which is easy to reproduce; it is, on the contrary, a permanent challenge which pervaded his work. In 1918, he wrote to Camoin: 'it seems that this is a paradise that we are not allowed to analyse and yet we are painters, for heaven sake. Ah! It's a beautiful place Nice! What soft and gentle light despite its glare. I don't know why I compare it to the light in the Touraine (there are perhaps two r's here). In the Touraine it is more golden, here it is more silver. Even the objects it touches are brightly coloured, like the greens, for example. Having written this declaration, I cast my eyes about the room where my pictures are hanging, and sometimes I think I've got hold of it, but it's not sure'.[41]

On 31st December, 1917, Matisse made his first visit

38. Fourcade, 178.
39. Quoted in Escholier, op. cit., pp.112–113, and in Fourcade, 122.
40. Fourcade, 122.
41. Fourcade, 109.

to Renoir in Cagnes. According to G. Besson, 'Renoir could not disguise his surprise at the apparition of this impeccable, sumptuous personage, a light felt-hat matching his ample shetland overcoat – a veritable manifestation of the "painter". Perhaps Renoir had pictured Matisse in terms of the legends which had grown up around some of the "renegades" from Montparnasse (Soutine, Modigliani . . .)'.[42] True to his usual custom, Matisse confirmed the social image he thought the painter should maintain, refined and cultivated, opposed to all notions of *laisser-aller* in the name of bohemianism or anti-bourgeois leanings; for Matisse, the seriousness of the work went hand in glove with respectability of appearance. Renoir, who was 76 years old (he died two years later), saw Matisse's first canvases from Nice: 'Everything is so right. It was difficult . . . That makes me angry.' Even if it is clear that these two artists worked in very different ways, a mutual respect quickly grew up between them. After Matisse's departure, Renoir said, with a laugh and a gesture as though he had an imaginary paintbrush on his leg, 'I thought that this fellow worked just like that . . . It's not true . . . He takes a lot of trouble!' (G. Besson). Doubtless Renoir too had fallen into the trap of thinking that the apparent ease with which Matisse painted was synonymous with facility; but he soon realized that this facility was merely superficial and was, in fact, the result of a prodigious work-process, obdurate daily practice with the resources of painting.

The years 1919 to 1929, known as Matisse's 'first 'Nice period', were rich in apparently 'easy' paintings: the *Odalisques* series, the still lifes, the luminous interiors all seem to be converging towards the expression of a profound serenity, a sense of happiness and of painting without problems. Through these paintings there came into being a quasi official version of Matisse as the expert

42. G. Besson, 'Matisse et Renoir, thirty-five years ago', cited by Escholier, op. cit., p.115.

Odalisque with Indian Trousers, *1925, lithograph.*
Print Department, Bibliothèque Nationale, Paris.

in bold colours, in subdued light and languid young women, which scarcely corresponds to the pictorial work he had pursued over the years, certainly calmer than the previous period on a first viewing, but nonetheless invested with a constant reworking of all that he had learned. To 'explain' how this period could have been regarded as an 'interval' in Matisse's work, critics have often pointed to the end of the war, and the sense of relief this would have brought to a painter nearing his fiftieth year. The result of this combination of 'the joyous years' and the special atmosphere of the Côte d'Azur, therefore, could have been seen as a new, slightly inferior version of *Luxe, calme et volupté.*

It is certainly true that Matisse's work at this time concerned itself hardly at all with misery. His starting point has nothing in common with – to take an example from the history of cinema which also reflects life on the Côte d'Azur – Jean Vigo, whose *A Propos de Nice*, an exposé of the other side of the leisurely life, dates from 1929. It is however untrue that this 'first Nice period' was entirely given over to the permanent exaltation of 'grace' and all that existence might offer that is immediately 'pleasant'. In fact, Matisse relentlessly questioned his own post-war achievements in the domain of colour, whose accords were becoming more audacious than ever while the painter permitted himself a return to the grey until recently prohibited. The same is true in the area of composition; here we see a certain perspective frequently taking over from the principle of pure frontality, constructing unusual angles of vision, and great complexity of space between windows and openings often duplicated by the inclusion of mirrors and paintings within paintings. Furthermore, the proliferation of decorative accessories (bouquets, floral or striped wall-hangings, tiles, carpets, etc.) demanded an extremely tight construction of the representative space, to the point where the female body could become, not the central motif, but just one form amongst all the others: less an exaltation of the female form, more an affirmation of the opposition of her curves to the horizontals and verticals (windows and balconies) and the obliques (curtains and carpets, perspective of furniture). In this way, the Odalisque theme condenses more than a memory, rather an 'impression' of Morocco, in which the costumes, the Moorish blind, the Arab hangings and carpets which recur in painting after painting, become symbolic or symptomatic accessories for the theatre of the mind which pays no heed to reality, but is entirely devoted to the elaboration of painting. The continual repetition of the theme, then, indicates not a lack of inspiration on the part of the painter, but his dedication to the exhaustion of all possible variations or combinations: 'To someone who said that I did not see women the way I painted them I replied "if I met a woman like that in the street, I would run away, terrified". After all I am not creating a woman, *I am making a painting*'.[43]

RECOGNITION IN FRANCE

These paintings, superficially more acceptable than *The Green Ray* or *The Dance* had a certain success: Matisse was beginning to be recognized by the French public. In 1918, he exhibited with Picasso (a new opportunity to confirm their reciprocal esteem: Matisse confessed to Max Jacob that, if he did not do what he did, he would like to paint like Picasso; Jacob replied that Picasso had said exactly the same thing). After 1919, the Bernheim-Jeune gallery began an annual exhibition of his most recent works. In 1922, the Luxembourg Museum purchased *Odalisque with Red Trousers* (p.115), and three years later Matisse received the Légion d'honneur.

On the occasion of the first Bernheim exhibition, André Lhote remarked that Matisse was now enjoying 'the success that so far the public had denied him', whilst deploring the fact that this success was obtained by his 'most superficial' works. Like many other critics, he stressed the 'unfinished' quality of Matisse's painting:[44] 'a Matisse canvas . . . stripped of details which in reality and in classical painting support the colour and disguise its technical significance, offers us the solution which is not complete but rather *in the process of being completed*. The artist makes us witnesses to his uncertainties by the "gaps", and to the feverish pace of his work by deliberately leaving pencil lines, smudges and stains on the

43. 'Notes by a Painter on his Drawing', *Le Point*, July 1939, Fourcade, 163.
44. Cf. Felix Fénéon: 'When confronted by a painting by . . . Matisse, people would object that it was unfinished – we would reply: at what moment is a painting finished? An unanswerable question . . . What is important, in that it is verifiable, is that the painting has been started, that is to say that its execution has been motivated by a problem of forms and colours, perfectly clear and pertaining only to the painting. In this sense, how many paintings which appear finished have, in reality, never been started.'

canvas'.[45] These remarks from André Lhote were later to be reversed for a certain pictorial modernity – which, in the United States as in Europe, would take for its goal precisely this affirmation of the autonomy of the painting with regard to its reference and everyday vision, and would take pains to show how what we know as 'painting' is produced on the canvas. This is clearly the case with Matisse, because it is only with the imposition on the eye of the not-yet-visible that the 'emotion' can be transmitted as the indefinitely present – and that the painting can find its true justification.

Simultaneously with his one-man exhibitions, the presence of his work in various Parisian Salons and exhibitions in other countries was confirming Matisse's international reputation. In 1920, he took part in the 12th International Art Exhibition of Venice, Signac being responsible for the French selection; in 1924 he was exhibited in New York, and had a retrospective in Copenhagen; in 1927 his work was shown in New York again, and 1929 at the Palais des Beaux Arts in Brussels.

At the beginning of the Nice period, Matisse was introduced to theatrical design when he conceived the decor and costumes for Stravinsky's *Nightingale* (performed by the Diaghilev troupe). 'The curtain, 18 metres by 15, consisted of a vast white rectangle on a black field with a yellow border on which were portrayed three masks and two buddha-like lions with green manes and vermillion breasts . . . The decor is pale blue with columns, the bases of which are the height of a man and are painted white. Enter sixteen dancers, carrying lanterns, and these lanterns, made luminous in this bluish milieu, not by electric bulbs but by the simple conflict between the vermillion painted on the outside and the lemon-yellow of the interior; besides, these yellow flowers, like stains on their costumes, what do they signify, if not splashes of light? This is only one example of the hundred ingenious, elegant and logical ways the artist expressed himself'.[46] Confronted with theatrical space and with real movement into which costumes had to be introduced, Matisse did not think for one moment to transpose one of his paintings. On the contrary, he took it as an invitation to experiment with new ways of inhabiting space, and to introduce into it symbolic colours which draw the axes and lines of force that sensitively reflect the choreography. The stage became yet another opportunity to examine the definition of space in terms of colours.

Also in 1920 an album of *50 Drawings* appeared, with a preface by Charles Vildrac (a second collection of *Drawings*, with a preface by Waldemar George, was published in 1925) and Marcel Sembat's little book inaugurating the collection of 'New French Painters' was published in the Nouvelle Revue Française. After this time, a reference to Matisse became obligatory in any history of modern painting. *Panorama de la Peinture Française Contemporaine* by Pierre Courthion (Kra, 1927), for example, devoted the chapter dedicated to colour to Matisse, thereby confirming his reputation as the greatest colourist of his time. While it is interesting to note, as Aragon did, that Matisse was ignored by Bénézit in the 1923 edition of the *Dictionnaire des Peintres, Graveurs, Dessinateurs* we should note that *La Revue Septentrionale* (a bulletin by the Rosatis in Nord-Picardie) took the opportunity to remark on the presence of a 'M. Henri Matisse (du Cateau-Cambresis)' in various salons and to mention the official purchases – in France and elsewhere – from which he benefited (we learn from the March 1935 issue that *Woman at the Window* was included in the French

45. André Lhote, *La Peinture, le Coeur et l'Esprit*, Denoêl, 1933, p.37. Twelve years later (the G. Petit exhibition), the same reproach was uttered by Gimpel: 'here we have thirty-five years of painting and not a single masterpiece; not a finished painting and the masterpiece is not to be found in the unfinished. The unfinished has prevented Matisse from enveloping his work with air, and masterpieces are drenched in it' (op. cit., p.434). One response to this, in addition to Fénéon's remarks above, is the comment Aragon wrote in 1972: 'Matisse used the *non-painted* as a value in itself' (*Ecrits sur l'Art Moderne*, Flammarion, 1981, p.268).

46. *Bulletin de la Vie Artistique* (Bernheim-Jeune gallery) no. 4, 15th January, 1920.

section of the Prince Paul Museum in Belgrade). It was probably necessary for Matisse to achieve an international reputation before his native Northerners were prepared to recognize him – since, in their eyes at least, he should not have abandoned the region of his birth; but this very act of desertion, the conversion of northern light into the light of the Midi, may not mean that he severed all emotional relations with his birth-place. Indeed, in 1933 his work was shown at the Rosati exhibition (Durand-Ruel gallery), and, more significantly he made a considerable donation of his work to the municipality of Cateau when the town expressed the intention of founding a museum in his honour.

However, resistance to Matisse had not altogether disappeared. Whereas Jacques Guenne, who published an important 'interview with Henri Matisse' in 1925,[47] estimated that *Odalisques* had saved the 1927 Salon des Independants from disaster,[48] *Le Crapouillot* deplored Matisse's return to 'the mish-mash of turkish carpets and bathetic odalisks . . . spitefully gnashing his teeth like an ex-revolutionary'.[49] One of Matisse's fiercest opponents was Camille Mauclair, a man ready to denounce the slightest sign of 'decadence' and particularly allergic to the odalisks which evoked 'cretonnes in the Place Clichy in the decor of a shabby turkish baths, stupid faces and inaccurate anatomy, bland and weak . . . a very able man who excels at not exerting himself. With supreme nonchalance he places a few versicoloured touches on the canvas, and he is so convinced that this is admiraable and definitive that he adds nothing else'.[50] A more positive indication of Matisse's reputation is to be found in John

Galsworthy's *A Man of Property*, in which Soames Forsyth, a collector who owns a Goya among other things, acquired a few Matisses 'before the war, because at that time people were making such a fuss about the Post-Impressionists'[51]: this 'fuss' would imply not only that British readers were aware of Matisse, but that they would also be able to appreciate the widsom of Forsyth's investment.

Figure opposite the Jar of Fish, *1929, etching. Print Department, Bibliothèque Nationale, Paris.*

Further confirmation that the twenties were anything but an artistic respite for Matisse can be seen in his output of sculpture and engravings (which were occasionally borrowed from compositions which first appeared as paintings). Between 1922 and 1929, Matisse produced one hundred and fifteen lithographs including *Odalisque à la Culotte Bayadère* (1925), one of his multi-technique masterpieces. In 1929 alone, he produced one hundred and eight engravings and dry-points, in which he re-examined solely by means of line and value all the formal problems which, in painting, could be solved by richness

47. Fourcade, p.79.
48. *L'Art Vivant* no. 57, 1st February, 1927.
49. Luc Benoist, *Le Crapouillot*, November, 1926.
50. Camille Mauclair, *La Farce de l'Art Vivant*, 'Nouvelle Revue Critique', 1930, pp.159–160. Whole passages from this work were reprinted in *La Crise de l'Art Moderne* (1944), in which Mauclair vituperously attacked Picasso, Max Ernst, Braque, 'Jewish' dealers and critics, as part of a general denunciation of 'degenerate' art. However, Matisse was spared on this occasion.

51. *A Man of Property*, trans. P. Michel-Cote, Calmann-Lévy, 1932, vol. I, p.96.

of colour. Several sculpted heads (*Henriette* II, 1927, and III, 1929) reveal an organization of space which had become increasingly free and yet all the more rigorous. And, in 1930, the fourth and final version of *Back* appeared, a monumental schematization in which the female form is summed up in a few vertical masses, transformed into a column which one senses is capable of supporting tremendous weight.

TAHITI, THE DANCE.

In 1927 Matisse received the Carnegie prize. Three years later he was invited onto the jury (which on that occasion awarded the prize to Picasso), but, for the moment, he spent only a short time in New York as a break in his journey to Tahiti (having originally thought of going to the Galapagos). New York delighted him; he even thought of working there in the long term: 'the space I sought unsuccessfully in Tahiti I have found in New York'.[52] The light in the city appeared to him 'so pure, immaterial, a crystal light'. He then travelled across the continent, visiting Chicago, Los Angeles and San Francisco.

He stayed in Tahiti for three months and painted only one canvas; but he did several drawings and took photographs which Matisse himself described as 'bad'. Stripped of all picturesque or exotic elements (as was his wont), a little blurred and lacking in originality (not unlike ordinary picture postcards), they served simply as souvenirs or aids to the memory, carefully annotated by their author to give an insight into his real interest: the breadth of the sea and the sky, the curve of the trunk of a coconut tree, the denseness of the vegetation. 'I lived for three months absorbed by the ambiance without a single idea in the face of the novelty before me, flabbergasted,

The Terrace of Hotel Stuart, photographed by Matisse.
'View behind my hotel from the terrace' (manuscript note by Henri Matisse on the back of the photograph above).

storing up so many things';[53] 'Each light offers its own particular harmony . . . The light of the Pacific, of the islands, is a deep goblet of gold which we peer into'[54] whereas our own is 'silver'. The light of the islands is nonetheless too constant, too stable to be truly inspirational: 'There the weather is fine from the moment the sun rises and does not change until evening. Such unaltered happiness is ultimately fatiguing'.[55] Matisse's days were taken up with sketching and swimming in the lagoons, accumulating sensations which were only later to be translated into material work. In Tahiti, he met the German film-maker, Mürnau, who was on location for his film *Tabu* and made two photographic portraits of Matisse. As usual, the painter took very little notice of the natives:[56] there was no question of seeking the ghost of Gauguin ('On the outskirts of Papeete, a colonial town with three thousand inhabitants, I found a little rue

52. Letter to Tériade, Fourcade, 108.

53. Note to Matisse in Escholier, op. cit., p.126.
54. In A. Verdet, *Prestiges de Matisse*, cited by Escholier op. cit., p.128.
55. Letter to Tériade, Fourcade, 125.
56. He was susceptible to clichés: 'The Tahitians are like children. They have no sense of what is prohibited, no notion of good and bad', Fourcade, 108.

Gauguin which had houses only on one side'[57]). Before leaving France, Matisse had sold *Jeune Homme à la fleur de Tiare* which he had bought some thirty years earlier, as a kind of symbolic break with the dead painter's work. 'In Tahiti, Gauguin only survives amongst painters "who endlessly recreate", encouraged by the inhabitants hoping to get their revenge', the same cliché: 'the sun setting over Moorea'.[58]

After a brief stay in France, Matisse returned to the United States, visiting Doctor Barnes in Merion, Pennsylvania. Barnes was the owner of an imporrtant collection of French paintings (including Cézanne, Renoir, Seurat), who wanted to commission the artist to decorate the hall which was to house the collection. 'Paint whatever you like, absolutely as if you were painting at home'. Matisse, who saw an opportunity to escape the strictures of 'canvas and easel' and to take on the challenge of what he was to call 'architectural painting', readily accepted – not realizing perhaps that the work would absorb him for the next three years.

The nature of the location proved to be a delicate problem to solve. An irrregular shape, it consisted of three semi-circles separated by arches supporting a vault situated in the half-light above french windows six metres high ('through which you could see nothing but lawn, only green with a few flowers and bushes; the sky was not visible'[59]), joined on the lower level by a long horizontal band. The total surface area was 52 square metres. The presence in the hall of other painters inspired Matisse to conceive his decoration in terms of something quite different from a simple enlargement of the usual canvas, as regards colours, composition and materials. 'It is a room for painters. To treat it like any other painting would be inappropriate. My aim was to translate painting into architecture, to make the fresco the equivalent of stone and cement'.[59] The shadow cast by the springs of the vault was to be integrated into the construction itself.

After working with maquettes, Matisse decided to start working to scale in a huge garage rented for the purpose. He rejected the traditional method of enlargement by squares because he considered that the inter-relationship between colours changed with quantity, and because he needed to take into account any deformations produced by the hanging of works in unusual places. Working on figures whose silhouettes were three metres high, he drew with charcoal fixed to a bamboo pole, and tried out his colour with pieces of paper covered in gouache paint and simply pinned to the wall to facilitate changes. Some ten years later, Matisse admitted that this technique, initially a functional expedient, could in itself generate self-sufficient plastic effects.

In this manner he completed a first version of *The Dance* (see p.121, a recurrent theme in Matisse since *La Joie de vivre* in 1906, which also gave rise to one of Shchukin's panels). Matisse immediately realized that the dimensions were incorrect and began work on a second version which was to be significantly modified. 'I had to change my composition (in terms of the different proportions of the gaps). The work itself had a different feeling: the first one is war-like, the second is dionysian; the colours are the same but are changed nonetheless'.[60] The final decoration was installed in May 1933 to the great satisfaction of both painter and patron. 'In my studio . . . it was only a painted canvas. In the Barnes Foundation it became something rigid, heavy like stone, and seemed to have been created at the same time as the building. . . . It is a splendour . . . the whole ceiling with its arches is alive with radiation and the same effect continues right to the floor'.[61]

The experiment was a success: Matisse remained con-

57. Matisse, in Escholier, op. cit., p.127.
58. Fourcade, 106.

59. Fourcade, 140.
60. Fourcade, 145–46.
61. Fourcade, 143.

Reclining Nude, *1927, and* Blue Nude IV, *1952.*

vinced that, from now on, painting could leave the easel behind, take on architecture and urban space and play a part in an environment far removed from the intimacy of the home. Here Matisse was approaching the preoccupations of the American Muralists, once again a step ahead of the tastes of the French public or officialdom.

The first version of *The Dance*, reworked after a trip to Italy (where Matisse went several times to see the Giotto frescos at Padua), was acquired by the Museum of Modern Art in Paris in 1937, at the instigation of Raymond Escholier (at the request of Madame and Marguerite Matisse, Cézanne's *Bathers* was added to the museum's collection). But unlike Léger, Dufy, Delauney and others, Matisse received no state commission for the 1937 exhibition. Nevertheless, he achieved a parallel triumph with fifty canvases assembled in two rooms to celebrate 'Thirty years of painting at the Petit Palais', which prompted Louis Gillet to assert that 'Matisse is the leader of the field, the master the most listened to and followed by the youth of today'. Gillet nonetheless complained that this work was only a 'Matisse stripped of its decorative function and of the loftiest and most generous fruit of his art and method' – notably in comparison with *The Dance* at the Barnes Foundation.[62]

The effects of this *Dance* can be identified in Matisse's painting over the following years, in a purifying of means: the rejection of the three-dimensional in favour of flat areas, a new affirmation of frontality to allow the motif to take its place more efficiently (more simply) in the visual space, the evolution of figures and decorative elements towards the radicality of the sign, allusive in its purity but sufficient to designate the form and volume. During these years, Matisse confirmed – with paintings as famous as *The Dream* (1935) or *The Romanian Blouse* (p.129) – that painting could be the equivalent of language (in its capacity to combine signs) and, at the same time, an invitation to the poetic dream – since, by their very schematization, the figures represented call on the observer to invest them with his own subjectivity.

BOOK ILLUSTRATIONS

In 1930, Matisse accepted an invitation by the publisher Albert Skira to illustrate an edition of Mallarme's *Poésies* which was to appear in 1932: a first incursion into 'book art' at which Matisse proved himself increasingly adept.[63]

62. Louis-Gillet, *Essais sur l'Art Français*, Flammarion, 1938, pp.143–149.
63. To the extent that, in the catalogue of 'L'Exposition des Artistes du Livre et de l'Imprimerie', held at the Museum of Decorative Art from 5th December, 1944 to 24th January, 1945, Matisse was listed simply as an 'illustrator-engraver'.

The book format provided another form of space to work with in terms of the successive deployment of pages, as much as the surface of each one. In the series of texts Matisse illustrated, there was no question of simply reproducing the meaning; he created a graphic transposition which could bring out certain latent connotations: 'The book should not need to be completed by imitative illustration. Painter and poet must act together, in parallel and without confusion. The drawing should be the plastic equivalent of the poem. Not first violin and second violin, but a concerted "ensemble" '.[64] Mallarmé's *Poésies* revived the first memories of Oceania, to be followed by *Pasiphaé* by Montherlant (147 lino-cuts), *Les Lettres Portuquaises* (15 full-page lithographs, 55 drawings), *Les Fleurs du Mal* by Baudelaire (one etching, 33 photo-lithographs and 33 initial letters on wood), *Repli* by Rouveyre (12 lithographs, 6 lino-cuts), *Florilège des Amours de Ronsard*, for which Matisse selected the texts (128 lithographs), *Poèmes* by Charles d'Orleans (100 lithographs), all providing variants on the Oceania theme. Matisse reserved total control over some of these (choice of paper, typography, space definition etc.) in order to define the legible-visible duality. He was aware of the presentation of his own lithographs, skilfully modulating the thickness of his line and the distribution of his colours. For him, the conception of a 'fine-book' was as noble as a painting, in that it could produce an authentically plastic space. Perhaps unique amongst these book-collectors' treasures were the engravings created for the first American edition of James Joyce's *Ulysses*. Matisse was more inspired by Homer's *Odyssey* than by Joyce's book (which he had not read), intuitively representing some of the generative themes of the novel; Ulysses putting out the eye of the Cyclops, in particular, inspired him to produce a cruel representation which is more or less unique in the totality of his work.

---

64. Escholier, op. cit., p.153.

Ronsard, Anthology of Love, *1948.*

The search for figurative space beyond the confines of the canvas went further than the book format; it can be seen in Matisse's designs for tapestries: the double version of *Window at Tahiti* (p.123), a design for *Nymph in the Forest* (p.127, which was never woven), or in studies in which we see the reappearance of gouache cut-ups, for the decor and costumes of *L'Etrange Farandole* (Monte-Carlo Ballet, 1937; music by Shostakovitch, choreography by Massine, who was responsible for the *Nightingale* in 1920): here there are echos of *La Danse* by Mérion.

A 'SECOND LIFE'

With the declaration of war in 1939, Matisse returned from Madrid (where he had been to see the masterpieces in the Prado) to Paris. For several years he had owned an enormous apartment in the Boulevard du Montparnasse. He had contemplated a trip to Brazil but the German invasion convinced him to stay in France, and the 'exodus' that followed took him – via Bordeaux, Ciboure, Saint Gaudens, Carcassonne and Marseille – to the Regina in Nice, and then to the villa 'Le Rêve' in Vence,

Matisse painting with charcoal on a bamboo stick. Nice, August 1949.

which he rented from 1943 to 1949. In January 1941, he underwent a serious intestinal operation from which he made a remarkable recovery. The nuns who nursed him described him as being brought back from the dead and from this moment on, Matisse felt he was benefiting from a 'second life'. His work expressed a kind of rejuvenation, attaining new heights of assurance and consummate simplicity.

Matisse worked feverishly during the war-years – no

The different states of the reclining nude, 1935.

doubt as a way of escaping from his anxieties about his family (Madame and Marguerite Matisse were involved with the Resistance and had serious problems with the Gestapo) or from 'professional' difficulties (he was approached about an 'official' visit to Germany and he refused; in 1942, during a series of radio interviews, he vigorously attacked the 'academism' of good taste of the epoch). The public image of Matisse, especially among his younger fellow-artists, was as a painter who represented *par excellence* the finest qualities of French art: audacity tempered by balance, the science of colour and composition. This image was confirmed by the number of forgeries in circulation during the war (an honour Matisse shared with Picasso, Miro and Dufy), and by the price levels attained by the public sale of his work in 1943–44. On a par with Delacroix or Renoir, a Matisse was worth ten times more than a Picasso (although it is true that, unlike the latter, Matisse had not been labelled a 'degenerate' artist). Goering appropriated various examples of French art, acquiring for his private collection *La Pianiste et les Joueurs de Dames* (1920), and a drawing *Odalisque aux Babouches* (1929).[65] It is not at all surprising that Aragon in his *Matisse-en-France* (1942) 'drafts one of those texts whose patriotism and literary heroism might today seem obsolete even though it belongs, with others, to the intellectual resistance of the moment'.[66] 'To paint well', Marcel Sembat advised him, is perhaps for an artist (especially at Matisse's age), the best way to prove his love of liberty and his patriotism: what disturbed him most was 'the uncertainty in which we live and the shame of submitting to a catastrophe for which we are not responsible. As Picasso said (referring to the French generals) "They are like the Beaux-Arts."

65. Exhibition Catalogue: 'Les Chefs d'Oeuvre des Collections Françaises Retrouvées en Allemagne par la Commission de Récupération Artistique et les Services Alliés', Orangerie des Tuileries, June–August, pp.19–20 and 59.
66. Laurence Bertrand Dorléac, op. cit., p.158.

If everyone did their job like Picasso and I do, all this would not have happened'.[67]

It was, in fact, on Picasso's initiative that a Matisse canvas figured in the 1944 Salon de la Libération and, in the following year, the two artists once more found themselves side by side at the Autumn Salon, then in December at the Victoria and Albert Museum in London, and again in 1946 at the Palais de Beaux-Arts in Brussels (27 works by Picasso, prefaced by Ch. Zervos, 24 by Matisse prefaced by J. Cassou). In January of the same year, the Maeght gallery in Paris exhibited canvases from the period 1939–41 accompanied by photographs showing the successive stages of their development (Matisse had been keeping photographic documentation since the thirties)[68] and revealing something of the painter's 'method'. The number of exhibitions was growing all over the world (Liège, Nice, Milan, Japan, retrospectives in New York, Paris, Lucerne). And Matisse was being increasingly honoured. In 1947, some of his important work was acquired by the recently opened National Museum of Modern Art; in 1950, he won the Grand Prix at the Venice Biennale (which he shared with the sculptor Henri Laurans). Alfred Barr's monograph *Matisse, his Art and his Public* for which Matisse designed the cover in cut-up paper was published. His paintings were seen in the large American museums thanks to a system of private donation. In 1952 the Matisse Museum was opened in Cateau. His work, available and renowned all over the world, was to become a touchstone for a growing number of European and American painters (from Motherwell to Sam Francis or Frank Stella).

In Nice and Vence, Matisse's 'second life' appears to have been comfortable – the décor was simple but refined, alive with green plants and cut-flowers, rich fabrics, knick-knacks, various *objets d'art* (from antiquity, from Africa, China, Oceania), with a population of up to three hundred birds. Physically, however, Matisse's life was extremely painful: since the operation, he had been obliged to wear a metal corset and could not remain upright for long periods. Consequently, with the aid of his assistant-secretary, Lydia Delectorskaya, Matisse

---

67. Letter to Pierre Matisse, 1st October 1940, Fourcade, 50–51.
68. Matisse's documentation of successive stages of his work is fully illustrated in Lydia Delectorskaya's *Henri Matisse . . . L'Apparente Facilité*, pub. Adrien Maeght, 1986. But it is also to be found in a far more modest work: *Matisse* by Georges Besson (Braun, (1950), which contains numerous photographs of works in states of completion which no longer exist (recognizable by the dates on the photos and the absence of signature). It is interesting to note that Matisse chose the photographs himself and supervised their presentation.

Matisse in his studio at Vence, 1944.

worked either sitting or lying down. During these years, his work attained an astonishing perfection, in its sureness and fluidity of line and in the way in which the white of the paper vibrates across the whole surface. (As Aragon wrote in 1942, 'I am quite prepared to say that a sheet of paper treated with Matisse's line is whiter than the virgin paper was originally'.[69] His 'sweep of line' was achieved over the course of prolonged study and extended periods of familiarization with the model – with the object, paradoxically, of 'liberating' the artist from it, allowing him, once having indicated his 'theme', to effect his series of astonishing variations, whether the departure point is a face, a body, a flower, a tree or whatever. 'For me, the model is a springboard, a door I must leap through to gain access to the garden in which I am so happy, so alone – even the model only exists for me to make use of it'.[70] If the model depends on a 'lightning bolt' (Aragon's phrase), Matisse himself needed to be so impregnated with it that his hand was free to work in a way he sometimes called 'unconscious' – work that had become so spontaneous that if he had to retrace a line left empty through lack of ink on the pen nib, 'however short it may be I cannot do it without trembling, without spoiling the sweep of the line'.[71] The 'progress' (Matisse's term) thus achieved ran the risk of tilting the balance in the 'eternal conflict between the drawing and colour' in favour of the former.

GOUACHE CUT-UPS

This conflict was to find its final resolution – leaving aside the post-war canvases – in the practice of gouache cut-ups, which began during the preparation of *Jazz*

Henri Matisse at Vence, 1944.

(started in 1943 and published by Tériade in 1947): Matisse discovered the possibility of drawing, with the use of scissors, in the colour itself. His assistants would cover sheets of paper with gouache, then the painter would cut them directly into shapes, without using a preliminary sketch – simultaneously defining contour and coloured surface. 'The scissors can take on a greater sensibility of line than the pencil or the charcoal',[72] and

72. A. Verdet, *Prestiges de Matisse*, Emile Paul, 1952, p.51.

'The Dream', Matisse's house at Vence, about 1944.

69. *Henri Matisse, Roman*, p.93.
70. Fourcade, 162.
71. Note by Matisse in *Henri Matisse, Roman*, p.82.

Matisse, Self Portraits, *1945, 1948, 1951.*

Matisse never tired of the pleasure he took in this work with 'paper-matter'. 'The cut-up paper enables me to draw into the colour. For me it is a question of simplification. Instead of drawing the contour and placing the colour in it – the one modifying the other – I draw directly in the colour, which is even more controlled in that it has not been transposed. This simplification guarantees a precision in the reunion of the two means which, from now on, are one and the same'.[73]

For the printing of *Jazz*, Tériade was obliged to order the manufacture of special inks. It was achieved using a stencil process, painstakingly reproducing Matisse's original colours – he had used gouaches which were no longer in production. The plates are interspersed with pages of bold manuscript whose function for Matisse was 'purely spectacular', but nonetheless charged with poetry. On its publication, *Jazz* was immediately greeted as a

radically new form of 'artist's book': the total conception of its author, using a technique which had only begun to reveal its possibilities, to bring together certain fundamental themes from his imagination (destiny, the heart, the swimmer, Icarus). He also reinvokes memories of Oceania in his decorative motifs (leaves, palms, the swimmer). With maturity, these memories return in force, allying themselves to the Mediterranean decor in a synthesis which was to pervade all future compositions in cut-up gouache. In Vence, Matisse found something of Tahiti: 'This morning, when I was walking in front of the house, watching the young girls, men and women rushing on bicycles to the market, I imagined myself back in Tahiti, at market time. When the breeze brought the smell of the woods or of burning grass, I could smell the woods of the Islands'.[74]

Up until 1949, Matisse produced cut-ups in a re-

73. A. Lejard (1951), Fourcade, 243.

74. Letter to Louis Aragon, *Henri Matisse, Roman*, vol. I, pp.187–188.

strained format with a single, simple motif (leaf, jelly-fish, coral, rosary, sea-weed), as if to create an elementary language which was to find its articulation in two linen prints (*Oceania, the Sea, Oceania, the Sky*) and two tapestries (*Polynesia, the Sea, Polynesia, the Sky*). Little by little, these combinations of simple motifs became increasingly important: photographs of Matisse's apartment show that he arranged them in real environments, leaning them against the walls and hanging them above the doors, making use of all available surfaces to animate the totality of the space and to constitute an enchanted 'life-frame'. Still wishing to develop his art in public space, Matisse envisaged the transcription of his larger compositions into ceramic (*The Swimming Pool*, 1952, was 16 metres long, the *Large Decoration with Masks* measured 10). Other pieces were transposed into stained glass (notably the last gouache cut-up, a *Rosary* commissioned by Nelson Rockefeller) – the work undertaken by Matisse in the chapel at Vence brought him to a serious study of the possibilities of this art which used light as a specific contribution.

LA CHAPELLE DE VENCE

If the gouache cut-ups can be regarded as the ultimate fruit of research in all areas of artistic production (Matisse remarked that 'cutting directly into colour reminds me of a sculptor's cutting directly into stone'), the Vence chapel incontestably represented the other side of the painter's genius as manifested in the years between the late forties and his death. At the time, not everyone understood the importance Matisse attached to this project (we know that Picasso suggested he should construct a market: 'You will paint fruit in it, vegetables . . .', to which Matisse replied, 'I don't care in the least about that: I have greens which are greener than pears, oranges more orange than pumpkins. So what's the point?'.[75] For Matisse, this was his 'masterpiece'. 'This project has taken four years of exclusive and assiduous work; it is the result of my entire active life. Despite all its imperfections

75. Fourcade, 268.

I consider it my masterpiece. Let posterity justify this assessment . . . even beyond the higher signification of this monument.' The text drafted for the presentation plaque expresses a similar sentiment: 'For me it is the completion of a lifetime's work, the fruit of an enormous effort which was difficult and sincere. It is not a work which I chose, but a work for which I was chosen by destiny at the end of my route, which I follow in accordance with my diverse researches, the chapel providing me with the opportunity to bring them together'.[76] Here, Matisse is anticipating, in the very vocabulary he employs, the way he later described 'having been called to his work as a painter' (see note 1) – which confirms his view of the chapel as a 'synthesis', combining the experiences of the long artistic path he followed. This is hardly surprising, if we remember that this path, parallel to his work on canvas, was characterized by a desire to attain an art-form which, in a space accessible to the public, can speak to everyone; that this desire should be realized in terms of a decorated architecture is entirely logical.

In 1941, after his operation, Matisse had the idea of constructing some kind of edifice as a gesture of gratitude towards the Dominican sisters who had nursed him. But it was not until 1957 that the project resurfaced. One of his former models, who had since become Sister Jacques-Marie, showed him a sketch for a stained-glass window she had conceived for the extension of the Dominican chapel at nearby Foyer Lacordaire. Matisse offered his advice, but soon formulated his own ambitious plans for an entirely new building, with the aid of Frère Rayssiguier, a student-architect, and Auguste Perret.

The chapel, consecrated in 1952, occupied Matisse for more than three years. He decided to take charge of all aspects of its development, the elements of worship as well as the architecture and decoration, in order to ensure the unity of the whole. The building is simple: the overall whiteness of the exterior is underlined by two small ceramics in an extremely sober black line drawing (a principle which recurs inside) evoking Saint Dominic and the Virgin and child. The only intrusion of colour is reserved for the roof on which the blue and white tiles (traditional colours of the Virgin) seem to reflect the movement of clouds across the sky. On the italianate roof there is a wrought-iron arrow more than twelve metres long: 'it does not crush the chapel but, on the contrary, gives it a height. Because I created this arrow like a drawing – a drawing I might do on a piece of paper – but this is a drawing that rises. When you see smoke rising from a cottage roof at the end of the day, and watch the smoke rising and rising . . . you get the impresssion that it does not stop. This is a little like the impression I gave with my arrow.'[77]

The interior decoration abides by the same demands of elevation and lightness, both physical and spiritual. Colour is restricted to 'an ultramarine, a bottle green, a lemon yellow' and is reserved for the stained glass, the ceramic murals being treated in black lines. But the diffusion of light through the windows, whose shapes (palms and leaves) Matisse perfected through numerous maquettes, produces a violet-pink coloration in the space itself and, depending on the time of day, enriches the drawn motifs with exceptionally subtle reflections. There is an omnipresent sense of the greatest simplicity: the faces of the Virgin and Saint Dominic are reduced to anonymous ovals stressing their universality; the panel depicting Virgin and child went through numerous stages before reaching its definitive version, in which the Virgin's robe (originally covered with stars) is left white, surrounded by clusters of clouds. We know that Matisse studied many classical Stations of the Cross before creating his own version which, instead of operating chronologically, presents the different stations on a single panel –

76. Fourcade, 257–58.

77. Fourcade, 266.

Interior of the Rosary Chapel, Vence. Left: The Virgin and Child
(ceramic); centre: The Road to the Cross *(ceramic), 1950.*

to be read in an ascending movement which conforms to the expressivity obtained by each stroke, and to the construction of the whole panel with lines of force which intensify its dramatic nature.

This was certainly the first time in the history of art (and of the Church) that a painter was given the opportunity to control an entire religious edifice and to supervise the unity of his project down to the last deteail:[78] as normal sacerdotal clothing would have disturbed the harmony of his colours, Matisse designed chasubles in which he could subtly combine elements of his own vocabulary with Christian symbolism; patiently working on every last item: ciborium and altar-cloth, chandeliers and crucifix, stalls and the door to the confessional, the altar itself and the paving of the floor. 'When I enter the chapel', he said to Father Couturier, 'I feel that it is my entire self which is present'.[79] The chapel represents a convergence of his skill with colour, his genius at drawing, and his cut-up gouache technique (which he had used extensively in the preparation of the stained glass and the holy orders), brought together to compose a total space, a volume both drawn and coloured, which instils the desired sensation of elevation in the minds and bodies of visitors. 'My chapel is not: *Brothers, we must die*. On the contrary, it is: *Brothers, we must live! . . .* I want visitors to the chapel to experience a lightening of the spirit. So that even non-believers will find themselves in a milieu in which the spirit is raised up, thought is clarified, and feeling itself is unburdened'.[80]

In 1943, Matisse had declared to Louis Gillet, 'I often say to myself that we profane life: through seeing things, we no longer look at them. We only bring dulled senses to bear on them. We no longer feel. We are blasé. I say to myself that to really appreciate something, it would be wise to deprive ourselves of it. It is good to begin by renouncing, to impose on oneself an abstention cure from time to time'.[81] In order to rediscover 'the near-religious feeling I have about life' (*Notes d'un Peintre*, 1908), Matisse restrained his palette for the Vence chapel, whose spiritual signification went beyond its Christian connotation. In the years that followed, he was to purify his technique even further in order to achieve a maximum density which, as Matisse admitted, prefigured the art of the future. 'As I create these coloured cut-ups, it seems to me that I advance joyfully to meet whatever awaits. I do not believe I have ever experienced such peace and harmony as in making these cut-out papers. But I know it will be many years before people understand how much what I am doing today anticipated the future'.[82] This is evident in *Sorrow of the King*; the series of four *Blue Nudes* (p.137), in which postures are reduced, by the treatment of the cut-ups, to a schema of essential lines; in *Souvenir of Oceania* (p.139), and *The Negress* of 1952, which used to be pinned to the wall of the apartment in such a way that the feet trailed across the floor, accentuating its dynamism. Some of these compositions border on 'abstraction' – as in the stained glass window in *The Bees*. 'I attained a form reduced to the essential and I conserved from the object, which elsewhere I had presented in the complexity of its space, the sign which is necessary to make it exist in its pure form and for the whole in which I conceived it'.[83] But in 1947, a period in which the figuration/abstraction debate was growing in France, Matisse maintained his distance from the distinction between the figurative and the non-figurative.[84] He declared that he did not understand the latter, although he did declare an interest in Kandinsky. 'Abstract art as we

---

78. Compared with the simple participation of Matisse (and Léger, Rouault, Bonnard, Lurcat, Bazaine) in the church at Assy; here it was simply a matter of elaborating on a pre-existing architecture. Matisse installed a version of Saint Dominic.
79. Fourcade, 273.
80. Fourcade, 266–267.

81. *Candide*, February 1943, quoted be Escholier, op. cit., p.208.
82. To André Verdet, in *2oième Siècle* no.35, 1970.
83. Fourcade, 249.
84. Letter to Rouvreyre, 25th December, 1947, Fourcade, 241.

understand it today seems to me to represent a dangerous tendency. It obeys the spirit of facility, "Abstract" artists do not connect themselves to anything, neither to themselves, nor to objects'.[85]

INEXHAUSTIBLE VISIBILITY

According to Matisse, all painting and, more generally, all art, should 'connect' to the artist and to his 'emotion' in terms of the world, and to that world itself, in which he will no doubt find only a pretext for sublimation, but one on which he must nevertheless lean. It is as if he is saying that the world, the visible, is in itself inexhaustible. When, towards the end of his career, Matisse began transposing people and objects into pure signs, it was in order to be able to perceive latent riches from a point of view that was increasingly 'innocent'. Until the death of the painter on 3rd November, 1954, the world offered itself up to him to be shaped by the grace of art. What importance would painting have if it could not represent, in its individual way, things that speech cannot express? To our know-ledge of the world must be added a sensual approach, the enigma of which cannot be reduced to concepts and ordinary language. If Matisse surrendered himself to this 'quite diverse and perverse personage who behaves differently with different people of whom he demands everything, and whose name is Painting',[86] it was surely because he expected a number of revelations from it, proving that everything remained to be done and redone in order to understand the unexpected, subtle opulence of the visible. This offering made by the world to the visual sense, its availability for the artistic act could be called *bonheur de vivre*, but only insofar as such *bonheur* implies a surprise and an unimaginable gift for the one who senses it. The gift offered by the world, as it effectively 'paints' before those who have been 'called', is reciprocated by the gift of the painting when the artist's work is accomplished. Such is Matisse's lesson, the combination of real modesty (that of the worker proud of his task) and of consummate generosity: others must be invited to share in the ecstasy generated by the inexhaustible visibility of the world.

85. To A. Lejard (1951), Fourcade, 252.

86. Letter to Aragon, 1942, *Henri Matisse, Roman*, p.207.

Henri Matisse at Vence, 1944.

THE PLATES

The Dinner Table, after De Heem, 1893

73 × 100 cm. Matisse Museum, Nice

Between 1893 and 1900, Matisse made a series of copies in the Louvre (Raphael, Poussin, Carrache, Philippe de Champaigne) to which he devoted some considerable time (six years on Chardin's *Ray*). De Heem's *Dinner Table* is significant for two reasons: at a time when eighteenth-century French painting (Fragonard, Chardin . . .) was enjoying popular success thanks to its promotion in the International Exhibitions, David de Heem provided Matisse with a model both for the treatment of values and for complexity in the construction of planes and volumes. But, above all, this 'Dinner Table' theme, initiated by a copy, was to recur periodically in Matisse, and developed in an increasingly original manner.

As for the 'fidelity' of the copy with regard to the original, Matisse himself stressed that this was entirely relative: 'The works which gained most favour before the purchasing commission (of the State) were those created by the mothers, wives and daughters of the museum-keepers. Our copies were accepted only for reasons of charity . . . I would like to have been able to produce literal copies like these mothers, wives and daughters but I was incapable of doing so. What was interpreted as boldness was simply the fact of experiencing difficulty in doing such and such a thing. This is why liberty is, in reality, the impossibility of following the path chosen by others; liberty consists in following the path your own qualities incline you towards' (Fourcade, 114–115).

The Dinner Table, 1897

100 × 131 cm. Private collection

Begun in the winter of 1896, just after the trips to Brittany, this canvas reveals a desire in Matisse to brighten his palette, at the same time demonstrating (in the treatment of the fruit and the glassware) an incontestable 'savoir-faire', capable of convincing the jury at the Salon (a jury which, nevertheless, only accepted *The Dinner Table* with extreme reluctance). It was left to Gustave Moreau to insist: 'No matter, his carafes are perfectly upright on the table and I could hang my hat over their stoppers. That's the essential thing.' In this painting there are three principal aspects which could have appeared shocking at the time: an affirmation of touch for its own sake (perhaps coming from 'Impressionism'), a form of composition which does not hesitate to truncate the foreground image giving a receding perspective to the laid table, and, above all, a use of colour which tends towards its own liberation. Thus, the stopper on the nearest carafe seems to contain the potential for an unfurling of Fauvist colours, and the reflections in the water in the second carafe owe nothing to the fruit in the bowl to the right.

'It was', recalls Matisse, 'a time when the terror of microbes was endemic. There had never been so many typhoid fevers. The public thought there were microbes in the bottom of my carafes!' (Fourcade, p.82). Picasso made a more professional comment, pointing out that light is not produced by white – something Matisse always remembered.

Orange Still Life with Indirect Light, 1899

74 × 93.5 cm. Private collection

Painted in Paris on his return from Toulouse, this painting resumes and condenses a series of works with the same theme which had been begun in Toulouse. Matisse is here affirming his intention to construct the canvas with colour, maintaining the memory of 'dazzlement' he felt in the South. The composition of the still life is, in itself, fairly traditional in the style of Vuillard and the Nabis, but the adoption of an elevated view-point serves to shorten the depth of field.

The composition is structured in coloured surfaces, at once contained and juxtaposed, each providing rich superimpositions of pigment and material. Although the motif is a modest one and its objects everyday, an impression of opulence and warm intimacy is generated by the colour – in particular by the orange which was soon to become the characteristic colour (or fruit) of Matisse.

Interior with Harmonium, 1900

73 × 55.5 cm. Matisse Museum, Nice

This canvas, like *Still life with Tureen* of the same year or *Madame Matisse as a Japanese* (1901), represents the period in which Matisse accentuated in his compositions the effects of perspective he began in *The Dinner Table* in 1897 (p.47), in order to emphasize paradoxes. Whilst the obliques of the harmonium define a 'hollow' representational space, to which the armchair-cover in the background also contributes, making the limits of the room recede outside the painted surface, the two pink flowers, on the other hand, are presented frontally, in the plane of the painting itself. Our perception is thus divided between a surface which presents only its flatness, and an illusory space within which the chair has difficulty in finding its rightful place: it is stabilized only by the gradations of colour at the rear, the gradations themselves placed in such a way that the angle between the floor and the wall is indiscernible, merely an impression of the curvature of space.

This conflict between the representational plane and the illusion of space has the effect of the chair becoming attached to the flower on the right, creating a kind of halo.

The constitution of a new perception of space preoccupied Matisse at this time to the point where figuration was stripped of all concern for detail: the objects are silhouettes fashioned by broad strokes which suffice to indicate their presence as masses. The problem was to place these masses in a space which creates its own pictorial homogeneity, and not copy the visible.

Matisse kept this painting most of his life, finally donating it to the Matisse Museum in Nice.

Luxe, calme et volupté, 1904

98.3 × 118.5 cm. Musée national d'art moderne, Paris

Since 1902, Matisse had been keenly interested in the work of Signac, whose earlier pointillism now admitted a broader, mosaic touch, although it still adhered to his principles on the decomposition of colour. It was, in fact, at Signac's house in the summer of 1904 that Matisse prepared *Luxe, calme et volupté*, originally entitled *Baigneuses* (a title more appropriate to Cézanne). It is his first great imaginary composition, which began in preliminary sketches detailing specific elements (the gulf of Saint-Tropez, the pine tree on the right), moved on to cartoons in the definitive size, and was finally transferred to canvas using the pounced drawing technique. All that remained was to add colour, for which Matisse chose to adopt Divisionist theories which, as he quickly realized, hardly suited his purpose, resulting in a difference in intention between the drawing (which 'depends on linear or sculptural plasticity') and the painting (which 'depends on coloured plasticity'). This gave rise to inconsistencies with the Signac position – theoretically forbidding recourse to line, clearly present in the painting, defining the bodies and the cups in the foreground – and certain *maladresses* (notably in the evocation of the clouds and a general stiffness of attitude).

Nevertheless, Signac obviously found the painting suitably convincing as he bought it; and it contains two fundamental aspects, critical to the future of Matisse's work: painting in mosaic style allowed a scale of bold colours, and above all, this first representation of the female nude (whose deliberately non-academic 'pose' is a challenge to the hypocrisy of official painting) ushers in a new area of subject matter concerning the happiness of a humanity which was originally 'innocent', a mythical 'golden age' where thought and feeling are mutually sustaining.

Woman with Hat, 1905

81 × 65 cm. Private collection

This portrait of Madame Matisse was one of the 'scandalous' canvases of the Autumn Salon in 1905. It is a portrait of a person whose context is familial intimacy, gloriously indifferent to the famous or official personages whose portraiture was already established as a tradition in modern art. Even more shocking to the establishment was its pictorial treatment, which must have seemed intolerably violent.

Freedom and thickness of touch suffice to construct a face and a bust simply in terms of their own oppositions without resorting to contour – the colour does the drawing – and independently of all local realism. The vigorous lines which construct the face (green underlining the forehead and the nose and, as in the other portrait of Madame Matisse from the same year *The Green Line*, dividing the face into a dark side and a luminous side; pink and pale green marking the jaw-bone) do not refer to anything of the 'real' but affirm the autonomy of the painting itself – note the complexity of the hat: a 'montage' of fruit and vegetables transforming it into a still life which only the presence of the arm and the upper part of the dress, forcefully asserted in neighbouring colours, prevents from becoming too independent.

The background on which the figure is inscribed is treated in broad strokes of the brush. Its diversified and equally non-referential coloration is due to the accordances established in the totality of the surface: the painting maintains only the flimsiest of relationships with the everyday visible, thus establishing a simple departure point to develop itself as 'pure' art – but it is capable of exciting in the observer an emotion comparable to that provoked in the artist's experience by the presence of his model.

Siesta at Collioure, 1905

59.6 × 73 cm. Private collection, Zurich

A perfect harmony of red, blue-green and pink, this interior scene uses materials sparsely, occasionally allowing the texture of the canvas to show through. The view onto the landscape is presented only through a shortened perspective transforming the little girl on the balcony into a kind of painting within a painting, while the miniature hanging above the bed is impossible to decipher.

The light is treated paradoxically: it enters the room in the normal way, through the window; but the walls are also invested with light produced by bright, non-realistic colours. The silhouette of the sleeper is anonymous and the lines of her face remain indiscernible as if she were sleeping in the shadows.

By this means Matisse transposes the effects of solar light through dark tones (the right-hand edge of the window and curtains), and the half-light with lighter tones. But the achievement of the colourist consists equally in the science of relationships between one colour-zone and its neighbours: the red of the dress is the same as the floor in the foreground but we can only verify this if we mask the colours that separate them. It is precisely because they are placed in relation to neighbouring colours (orange and pale tones for the dress, more sustained colours for the floor) that they appear different to the eye.

The Red Carpets, 1906

89 × 116.5 cm. Grenoble Museum

In Matisse's work, paintings in which fabrics play a foreground role are extremely numerous: he was fascinated by their motifs, but also by the disharmony which their juxtaposition might create and the consequent necessity to transcend it. That said, in this painting, he did not succeed – especially as the objects integrated into the composition (plate of fruit, melon etc.) assert their autonomous presence (in the catalogue, Matisse at the Grenoble Museum, published in 1975, D. Fourcade remarked that the plate of fruit 'is a fauvist unity all by itself'); while, on the other hand, the carpet presents a frontality or a 'flatness' which, although it corresponds to the general direction taken by Matisse's technique at this time, is not exploited here since, even if the carpet hanging on the wall is truly 'flat', those draped on the couch are presented in perspective, hollowed in folds, re-creating an illusory space in the painting.

The chromatic gamble in this composition clearly depends on the co-existence of different reds and different greens – and its success is less than assured. Nevertheless, the dissemination of points of colour on the horizontal carpets succeeds in unifying them through a kind of exchange of their separate qualities.

La Joie de vivre, 1906

The Hart Collection, U.S.A.

This is one of the many preparatory works for the painting with the same title – the largest composition undertaken by Matisse thus far (174 × 238 cm). The piece shown here was done in coloured pencil and is particularly elaborate. A sketch (Copenhagen Museum), painted in broad mosaic touches, confirms that the landscape represented was originally painted from life, later refined properly to accommodate the figures in their own space: figures which refer to a scene reminiscent of cultural mythology or the mythology of dreams (the Golden Age). In this, and in its extensive exploitation of the nude, it recalls *Luxe, calme et volupté* (p.53).

This pastoral, bringing together as it does, allegories from the arts (music and dance) and from the pleasures (physical beauty and love), reverberates with multiple echos, as much literary ('Daphnis and Chloë' or Virgil) as pictorial (Moreau or Ingres): from this point of view, the signification of the composition is too heavily cultural to be original. Its strength, in fact, lies in its formal treatment, in which is expressed the painter's appropriation of myth: the primordial importance of the sinuous arabesques which unify figures and landscape, the role of the outlines defining the two reclining figures at the centre of the picture, whose validity is more to do with the overall organization of the surface than with anatomical considerations, the boldness of colours (great flat areas of colour on the canvas) and the diversity of poses, all contribute to evoke an impression of happiness at once desirable and lost, of an archaic innocence forever out of reach. This Golden Age, as part of Matisse's subject matter, returns later in his painting, specifically in the works for which *Joie de vivre* serves as matrix – notably in terms of the dance sketched in the distance (see pp.63, 67, 73, 87).

Blue Nude (Souvenir de Biskra), 1906

92 × 140 cm. Baltimore Museum of Art

Using a central figure from *La Joie de vivre*, this is one of the most violent canvases painted in 1906: the choice of blue (reiterated extensively in *Blue Nudes*, 1952, p.137) combines with the torsion imposed on the body to create an 'erotic' ambiance which is further accentuated by the agitated, almost convulsive nature of Matisse's touch. In addition, the corrections to the anatomy remain visible, forming a halo which projects the nude towards the observer, even if the face seems to be expressing a certain reserve.

Only the decorative palm-trees and fig-leaves in the distance (the only place where colour is allowed to shimmer luminously) justify the parenthetical sub-title – but it reveals that this canvas crystallizes two Matissian themes: the elaboration of the Eden myth and the use at a later date of memories of his travels.

In 1907, Matisse completed several sculptures based on the same *souvenir*, which, between 1908 and 1924, feature in at least nine paintings.

Self Portrait, 1906

55 × 46 cm. Statens Museum for Kunst, Copenhagen

Matisse had worked extensively on self-portraits – though rarely on canvas – observing himself in the mirror as he would any other model, seeking to generate the same responses as in any other work: emotion and interiorization.

This canvas is the product of the same aesthetics as its contemporaries: frankness of colour, swiftness and authority of touch, the use of green to define the forehead, nose and cheek as in the portraits of Madame Matisse (1905, p.55). But here we have one of the few representations of Matisse in 'casual' dress, the sailor's vest being a holiday souvenir, serving to give the face the air of an audacious explorer.

What is being asserted in this self-portrait, from the point of view of the artist himself, is, firstly, an unfailing will: the head has a sculptural power; its energy is concentrated in a look which sternly summons the observer, stubbornly defiant of all adversity. At the same time, this painting brings together a number of allusions to other works in the history of art (from Byzantium to Cézanne), carving its own place in their continuum by going one stage further. Matisse's kind of modernity is not a simple, destructive negation of what has gone before: only by assimilating the past could he be free of its influence.

Le Luxe I, 1907

210 × 138 cm. Musée national d'art moderne, Paris

First exhibited at the Autumn Salon and functioning as a sketch for the second version of 1908, *Le Luxe I* was completed at Collioure in the summer of 1907 using the same classical techniques as in *Joie de vivre* and the still earlier *Luxe, calme et volupté* (preparatory drawings and charcoals, also to be found in the Museum of Modern Art Collection, then pounced or dotted technique for the transfer to canvas). This return to an academic treatment coincides once again, in a large-scale work, with an exploration of the nude, accomplished here under the dual patronage of Gauguin and Puvis de Chavanne: in fact Matisse's Fauvism is also a matter of settling scores with his masters – showing that the use of a different form can breathe new life and meaning into their themes.

The three female figures at the seaside are participating in the same paradisal ambiance to be found in *Joie de vivre*: ecstasy beyond history, by dint of attitudes and movements, euphoria of colour. The monumentality of the work is achieved not only by its physical dimensions: it is more a question of simplicity and balance, of osmosis between figures and landscape, and of the equivalent plastic presence of all points on the surface.

The Red Dining Table, 1908

180 × 22 cm. Hermitage Museum, Leningrad

The 'dining table' motif of 1897 (see p.47), already present in *The Brittany Servant* of 1896, here undergoes a radical transformation: the theme is only a pretext for the deployment of arabesques and pure colour – freed from all verisimilitude by the contamination of a fabric which uniformly covers both wall and table (whose volume in the foreground is indicated only by the curves of the motif) in such a way that the space of the room is transformed into a wall of paint. In relation to this, the landscape in the window-frame opens up no depth whatsoever as it is, itself, treated frontally – to the extent that one might easily see it as a painting within a frame. In this general disposition where the servant herself is merely a configuration of curves, responding to the movement of the trees, her dark blouse balancing the weighty intrusion of the green of the landscape, specific points of colour introduce a sense of rhythm to particular areas (the yellow flowers in the field are continued in the vase, the triangle of the vase-stand, the carafes and the fruit all repeat the same colour, while the ochre of the servant's hair reflects that of the chair), which creates a counterpoint to the large 'S' motifs of the fabric.

This *Red Dining Table* has two antecedents: the first was painted in a rather cool green; the second, in blue, (the original colour of the Jouy canvas used as model) was bought by Shchukin and exhibited as *Harmony in Blue* at the Autumn Salon of 1908. This evolution of the painting clearly demonstrates that for Matisse the unity of the work is achieved, not by coherence of representation *vis-à-vis* the everyday, but by construction through formal rhymes and agreements of colour.

Still Life, Blue Cameo, 1909

88 × 118 cm. Hermitage Museum, Leningrad

The cloth which serves here as background for the still life is the same – before transformation – as the one in *Red Dining Table* (see p.69), for which this canvas constitutes a kind of annexe – but its motif is treated in a particularly full manner.

Following a device that Matisse used in several paintings of this period, the surface of the cloth designates, without fold or break, both the vertical wall and the horizontal surface, creating a curved space onto which the objects of the still life are incrusted without projected shadows – thereby giving equal importance both to the background and to the still-life elements, whose colours are adjusted in accordance with the necessary harmonies (for instance there is nothing 'metallic' about the chocolate pot).

Thus the sense of perspective is evoked by subtle allusion, by the deformation of the motif in the lower half of the painting – and by the angle of the cloth on the right of the canvas, which is further invoked by the difference in colouring between the wall and the table: no sooner has the eye been distracted by this escape from the printed motif, than it is immediately recaptured by it and is forced to confuse the two canvases (printed and painted) in the same frontality.

The Dance, 1909

259.7 × 390.1 cm. Museum of Modern Art, New York

The first version of one of the panels commissioned by Shchukin on which Matisse commented: 'There are three stages. I imagine the visitor who comes from outside. The first stage is offered to him. We must obtain an effort, we must give him relief. My first canvas represents *The Dance*, this round in full flight at the top of the hill'. The second stage was to be 'a musical scene with attentive characters', the third, 'a scene of relaxation' which was to become *Bathers by a River*, p.101 (*Les Nouvelles*, April 12th, 1909).

This round is an enlargement of the one which occurs in the background of *Joie de vivre* (see p.61), which marks a return to painting concerned with the primordial and the 'sacred'. The original six figures have been reduced to five, accentuating the dynamic of the oval that forms the bodies, and thereby introducing a tension which is emphasized by the gap between the two hands described on the strongest diagonal (right arm, then left arm, bust and right legs of the two nearest figures). The three colours, broadly brushed to maximum intensity, underline the dionysian signification of the composition – while the canvas shows through here and there in the outline of the figures, sustaining a sensibility we might call tactile which was to disappear from the second version.

In this way the myth is brought closer, and suggests what Pierre Francastel has called 'an immediate poly-sensational experience': sight and movement, but also the primal music of the hammering of feet on earth. In closing their ritual circle, these figures are asking the observer to put his own energy to the test.

Purple Cyclamen, 1911

73 × 60 cm. Acquavella collection, New York

Nothing could be more banal than the theme of this painting: a pot of flowers on a garden table ... but simplification and the exaggeration of form and colour transcend the motif as they bring to light a series of contradictions which turn the canvas into a field of strongly opposed tensions.

Here, the perspective of the oval of the table is contradicted twice over: by the frontal representation of the cyclamen, but also by the division of the background into coloured zones with no representative allusion. Besides which, the pot, the table-top and its base are designated by surfaces which remain two-dimensional in a way that tends to draw them into the background. Only the plant has the benefit of a relatively precise figuration, its development designed to oppose the flatness of the other forms. Balance is thus achieved both by the colour scale and by the way in which the initial layers of colour are visible beneath the later brush strokes and also by the equal importance attached to all points on the surface: seen in this way, the manner in which the two green circular zones accord with the flowers across the blue is essential.

The Red Studio, 1911

181 × 219.1 cm. Museum of Modern Art, New York

Any view of the inside of a studio is, traditionally, the privileged moment when the artist states the specific characteristics of his art. *The Red Studio* is part of this tradition and derives maximum effect from it, a masterful exposition of the two governing principles in Matisse's work in 1911: the painting is (only) a surface independent of everyday reality and its perception; it is colour that must impose its order on this surface.

The studio is a hermetic place, with no escape into the outside world and uniquely consecrated to art: thus the constitution of the catalogue presented here – sculpture (*La Serpentine*); ceramics (the plate decorated with a nude in the foreground, with its five-petal motif reiterated, not only in *Nude with White Scarf* of 1909 which features here but was later destroyed, but also over the entire surface of *Interior with Aubergines* (see p.81)); and painting (*Luxe II*, *Purple Cyclamen*, *Sailor*, *Nymph and Faun*) all recreated in the two-dimensional form of the image and, in each case, interpreted as a function of the dominant colour. To this are added the tools of the trade (easels, frames, stools) all dominated by the red which invades the canvas and devours them since they are painted only in outline, as is the furniture and the lines of perspective: sketched in this way, these lines are reduced to a mere memory over which the colour will always prevail, an expression of the serene jubilation of someone who is able to reproduce with assurance a universe which remains forever autonomous and incontestable and over which his mastery is complete.

The Conversation, 1911

177 × 217 cm. Hermitage Museum, Leningrad

Although apparently influenced by Byzantine art in its choice of blue, green and red tints, and the way these colours saturate the picture, this canvas was completed in 1911, before the trip to Moscow where Matisse was to spend many hours studying icons. We must assume, therefore, that the Byzantine references in this painting were a result of Matisse's visits to the exhibitions of Byzantine art in 1913 (Paris) and 1918 (Munich). The apparent subject is once again trite and bourgeois: the painter and his wife in the privacy of their home in the morning. But this is transcended by the formal organization of the canvas where, time and again, straight lines are opposed to curves (the man and the woman, the window-frame and the balcony, the tree-trunk and the solid masses of colour), creating a unifying structure over and above the two figures.

The window occupies the central space, 'interrupting' the conversation by offering a view onto the place where the painting was executed (the studio at the bottom of the garden). Art imposes silence because it is the modern form of the sacred; Pierre Schneider, pointing out that, in its composition, this canvas superimposes classical echos (from *The Arnolfinis* by Van Eyck to Fra Angelico's *Annunciation*) could justifiably consider it a 'modern icon'. 'What we might call the religious feeling for life' which Matisse possessed, confirms the ambiguous nature of all that is sacred: it attracts and fascinates like the landscape offered through the opening in the blue, but, simultaneously, it implies terrifying demands – like those imposed on Matisse's life at this time, when he suffered from a series of anxieties, insomnia and family problems.

Interior with Aubergines, 1911

212 × 246 cm. Grenoble Museum

In this key work, Matisse summarizes all the research of the period, when he was working towards a kind of painting that would be nobly decorative, that is to say, capable of bringing together an oriental sense of decoration (see p.59) and western concerns for realism. *Interior with Aubergines* presents itself to the eye with such evident conviction that it is necessary to decompose the elements in order to fully appreciate the audacity with which Matisse stretches to the limit the formal and compositional contradictions.

The unity of the painting – and also the sensory impact, equal in all its constituent parts – is ensured by the abundance of decorative elements (the fabrics, the arabesques on the screen, and the giant clematis which subsume the surface in a way contrary to any realistic perspective, and are ultimately framed on the left as if in a separate painting) which compete for attention with the central still life (itself a subject sufficient for any traditional painting). Even though 'flatness' is assured by the five-leaf motif, Matisse permits himself an ironic reflection on the classical construction of space with the introduction of motifs, but the landscape painting represented in the window refuses to admit any illusory 'hollowness'. The articulation of planes and surfaces is both complex and blurred, by rhyming of colour in specific places, but also by the mirroring of a simple variant of the still life. It is equally remarkable that the landscape on the right is not continued in the opening indicated behind the screen.

The composition, therefore, is implicitly defined as a continuous battle between surface and depth, concern for realism and decorative ambition. Originally, this work was surrounded by a border (17 cm wide) in which the clematis motif was reinforced – later to be removed by Matisse, who may have regarded this as too clear a victory for supporters of the decorative.

Goldfish, *1911*

147 × 98 cm. Pushkin Museum, Moscow

As with flowers and plants, goldfish form a constant theme in the work of Matisse: their presence in a transparent bowl symbolizes the liberty of colour in relation to the material nature of common objects and physical bodies, and at the same time underlines the equal value of surface and representation.

At a point starting with the red stripes which indicate the fish, the 'emotion' so dear to the painter is diffused through their approximate reflection in the surface of the water, then through the successive circles representing the circle of the table, which also indicate the curve of a bench or garden chair on the left, and finally the coloured effervescence of the flowers on the right-hand side of the canvas.

The plunging perspective again permits (see p.51) a destabilization of the pictorial space, so that background and foreground retain equal importance.

The Blue Window, 1912

130.8 × 90.5 cm. Museum of Modern Art, New York

In classical painting since the Renaissance, an open window has always provided the possibility of opening the representation onto an exterior space in which the illusion of perspective is sovereign. To achieve this, it is obviously necessary that the window be perceived as such, that is to say, inscribed in the composition like a hole in the materiality of a wall. This is what is happening, in a rather particular manner, in *The Conversation* (p.79).

Here Matisse stresses the continuity between interior and exterior to the extent that the bay of the window becomes invisible, existing only as a black strip – we are in no way obliged to interpret this as a window-frame since, graphically, it forms part of the tree.

The dominance of blue, reinforced by the vertical band on the left suspends all sense of perspective. Echos of colours and forms force the space inside and the space outside to communicate: the ochre of a distant rooftop is mirrored four times in the interior; the globe-like branches correspond to the circles of the red flower, the place-mat and the plate; the decoration on the vase on the left harmonizes with the fan of branches to its right.

Such a device communicates more than just the homogeneity of space; it conveys the capacity of the mind not simply to perceive things in isolation, but rather, as Matisse had learned to do, to comprehend the relationship that exists between them.

Nasturtiums and 'The Dance', 1912

190.5 × 114.5 cm. Pushkin Museum, Moscow

In 1909, Matisse integrated the first version of *The Dance* (p.73) into a luminous *Still Life with 'The Dance'* (Hermitage Museum, Leningrad), the first time he incorporated part of his own output in one of his paintings. In this painting, Matisse takes evident pleasure in 'anthologizing' (see *The Red Studio*, p.77), stating an equivalence between art and reality in terms of 'motifs'. He was becoming increasingly aware of the possibilities inherent in 'variants' on his canvases.

Placed obliquely against a wall, *The Dance* loses the sacred nature which its original frontality conferred on it – a loss confirmed by the way in which the stool and the nasturtiums, whose ordinariness contradicts all allusion to the Golden Age, disturb the image, while the chair in the foreground revives the comparison of painting (and therefore of *The Dance* itself) to a 'good armchair'. This 'secularization' of the theme permits a different version, from which the evocation of the earth has significantly disappeared, and in which the bodies have become more supple, but imbued with a 'kinetic' effect produced by the traces of corrections left on the canvas. The memory of the painting (itself duplicated, since any changes to this representation of *The Dance* apply simultaneously to *Nasturtiums with 'The Dance'*) alters with that of the movement represented.

Portrait of Madame Matisse, 1913

145 × 97 cm. Hermitage Museum, Leningrad

Possibly started in 1912, this portrait required more than a hundred sittings in the garden at Issy-les-Moulineaux. 'The perfect example of the work-event', according to André Breton who, although he had not seen the painting since the Autumn Salon of 1913 where it was a great success, retained a very precise memory of it some forty years later. It was purchased by Shchukin.

Unlike previous portraits (notably *Woman with Hat*, 1905, p.55, or *Self Portrait*, 1906, p.65) this canvas insists on the decorative aspect of painting (harmony of colour, the sinuosity of the scarf, feathers in the hat) putting the psychological dimension into suspension. The face is almost an enigmatic mask, with its lifeless eye-sockets, the black underlining of the eyebrows, nose and mouth – a hint of the influence of African works (Matisse, along with Derain, Vlaminck, Picasso and Braque, was one of the first western artists to collect pieces from Africa, without using them as obviously as the Cubists to create a new form of representation).

The 'abstraction' of the face, which Matisse was to take up again towards the end of his career in certain drawings and cut-up gouaches, is accompanied by an impression of gentleness. There is a rigorous chromaticism in the portrait and something hieratic about the pose; the slight inclination of the head is sufficient to give it a sense of proximity, corresponding to the intimacy between artist and model. This is the last portrait Matisse painted of his wife and, in its blend of flair and restraint, is certainly the most moving.

Still Life with Oranges, 1913

94 × 83 cm. Louvre Museum, Picasso donation

Present in numerous canvases since 1896, orange is Matisse's principal colour support (i.e. for surface and visuality), a long way from the colour-values with which he served his apprenticeship, copying Chardin and David de Heem (see p.45). But it is also, to borrow Pierre Schneider's expression, 'the botanical emblem of the Golden Age', evoking natural plenty and implicit sensations of taste.

Painted in Tangier, *Still Life with Oranges* confirms that, in Morocco, Matisse had rediscovered a direct contact with nature – the natural dispenser of an opulence which demands to be transposed into pictorial terms. The articulation of forms in this painting is particularly subtle – notice the false symmetry of the curtain and the glass door – as is the range of colour. In the drawing, the basket of fruit is given less priority than the bold design of the fabric. In the finished work, it assumes an altogether different importance, by virtue of the greater detail and by the way in which the table-cloth rises to meet it at the centre of the picture. Conversely, in the drawing, the surrounding white played a dynamic role, which is performed in painting by the allusive treatment of space.

Picasso, who bought this painting during the war from a German collector, considered it to be the most precious Matisse in his possession.

French Window at Collioure, 1914

116.5 × 88 cm. Musée national d'art moderne, Paris

Dating from a period particularly rich in important works, this canvas is perhaps the most exciting – in that, at first sight, it could seem entirely 'abstract' consisting, as it does, only of coloured verticals. (When exhibited in the United States in 1966, it was greeted as the precursor of certain minimalist works.) Nevertheless, Matisse maintains a sense of depth in the representation, by means of the obliques in the bottom of the picture, the differing intensity of the black (from which we can infer the presence of a floor), and the scoring on the left, which indicates the reality of a blind.

In its original state, the french window gave onto an exterior landscape, covered during the last work session with a wash of black, which blots it out, thus signifying the dazzlement created by excessive light (recalling Eliphas Levi's formula, 'the foolhardy person who dares to look at the sun without shade goes blind and therefore the sun for him is black'). This blindness coincides with a tendency towards over-simplification particularly apparent in works of the war-years. Above all, it stresses that the strongest light can be rendered by its apparent opposite (see p.105). This inversion of values, in which interiors are brightest, underlines the fact that the french window has a differentiatory function – unlike what happens in *The Blue Window* (1912, p.85). Furthermore, the almost exact coincidence of the subject with the format of the canvas, affirms that what we are observing is no landscape; it is a painting.

View of Notre-Dame, 1914

147.3 × 94.3 cm. Museum of Modern Art, New York

This canvas, in which the successive lines of construction are left visible, is certainly the most developed of all the works in which Matisse sought to geometrically schematize his motif. If the right-hand margin indicates the upright of a window, the two horizontals and the truncated vertical are much more ambiguous, even though their presence, like that of the two obliques, is necessary to balance the finished design of the cathedral, whose mass and light are imposed in the upper part of the painting.

The schematization is not confined to forms; colour is likewise reduced to a blue, spread practically over the whole surface, independent of all verisimilitude.

Taken to extremes, this process of simplification would achieve no more than the aesthetic of the wall-poster. However, emotion is here maintained precisely by the way in which the process remains inscribed in the work; in the half-erased lines, in the light colours beneath the surface visible through the blue, and in the irregularity of the finally definitive lines: instead of creating a canvas from which all trace of the development process has been removed, Matisse leaves exposed the successive stages of this process, giving the observer the opportunity to reconstruct the separate moments in this development.

The Yellow Curtain, 1914–15

146 × 97 cm. Stephen Hahn collection, New York

The window suspended *The Conversation* (p.79), by revealing the very place where the painting was being realized at the same time as its departure point in nature. Matisse had also experimented with it as a transparent passage between exterior and interior (p.85) or, conversely, as a possible zone of blindness (p.93). Here it has been transformed into the metaphor most appropriate to painting itself, exposing the specific dialectic which brings artistic creation together with its natural subject matter: if it is true that nature gives rise to art, it is also true that, thanks to painting, nature's most secret riches are unveiled.

The starting point for *The Yellow Curtain* is the garden at Clamart, reduced to a minimum of elementary forms. But just as important is the almost exact coincidence between the window and the canvas itself. The framing of the one provides the borders of the other, to the extent that, if it were not for the curtain and the two horizontal traces of an erased balcony, one could quite easily confuse the two. In fact, for Matisse, both have the fundamental capacity to bring something of the visible to the field of emotion and perception. Given that this has been refined and reduced, it indicates how painting can outstrip ordinary appearances, imposing its own laws upon them, or in other words, the extent to which pictorial (cultural) elaboration may be developed in relation to a natural phenomenon. For Matisse, this will never be total non-figuration, even though he gets close to it in *The Yellow Window* and *French Window at Collioure*. However, it would be a mistake to deduce that in terms of painting it is sufficient to ask the question 'What to paint?'. The real question, and the one which lies behind Matissian painting, is more subtle: how to elevate a chosen object (place, body, face, etc.) to authentic pictorial status without totally eradicating all reference to the non-painter's perception?

Goldfish and Palette, 1914–15

146.5 × 112.4 cm. Private collection, New York

A discreet example of Matisse's 'Cubist' phase (1914–17), reflecting the painter's solitary assault on the last remaining formula of the *avant-garde*, *Goldfish and Palette* exemplifies many themes and objects characteristic of the beginning of this process. First we have the view of the studio, where the painter's presence is merely ghostly, reduced to a single thumb-print on the palette. Then there are the window – opening onto a non-specific exterior; the studio, being the place *par excellence* where the painter can express himself in an autonomous manner; the goldfish, reduced to simple spheres; the bowl in which the water is simultaneously opaque (the black background is occluded) and transparent (the fish and the green leaves are visible); the arabesques of the balcony balancing the diverse diagonals and the large vertical black strip.

If we compare this canvas with *Goldfish* (1911, see p.83) it is clear that the emotive charge is very different: it provokes a sense of oppression, confirmed by a general impression of suffocation, despite the clarity of the bowl and the colours of its immediate surroundings. Should we see this as a true influence of Cubist painting – noted for its indifference to brilliant chromaticism? It would be equally valid to interpret it as a reflection of the depression of the war-years.

Variation on a Still Life after David de Heem, 1915

180.9 × 220.8 cm. Museum of Modern Art, New York

The fourth important appearance of the dining-table theme (see also pp.45, 47 and 69), this canvas, which stylistically recalls the adherence to Divisionism seen at the time of *Luxe, calme et volupté* (p.53), in a sense defines the limits which Matisse imposed on his borrowing from Cubism, and doubtless reflects the long discussions he had with Juan Gris in Collioure in 1914.

A cursory comparison with the 1893 De Heem copy (p.45) reveals a significant restructuring of the framing of the motif, accompanied by a change in the format; we should further note that the original still life objects reappear, with minor exceptions (a glass between the two vases has disappeared, certain specific arrangements have been reduced – the absence of a fruit, or a bit of peel here or there . . .). But it should be pointed out that 'Cubist', geometric construction is present only in the space surrounding the objects and is in no way concerned with the objects themselves, which, instead of being viewed from all sides in an orthodox manner, present to the observer only the surface he would normally see. Thus, the verticals, obliques and curves which scan the background and the table supporting the still life exist only as exaggerations of the lines suggested by the arrangement of the decor, and it is significant that they do not disturb our perception of the object (a diagonal brushes against the glass on the right, taking great care not to obfuscate the form). What Matisse retains (or accepts) from Cubism is that which corresponds to his own direction: the simplification of forms, the complexity of spatial construction, the importance of flat colour surfaces. But once again, the canvas must generate an authentic emotion – in which geometry will play only a supportive role; Matisse vehemently refused to make it an end in itself.

The Piano Lesson, 1916

245.1 × 212.7 cm. Museum of Modern Art, New York

A composition of austere monumentality, *The Piano Lesson*, takes its apparent subject matter from an intimate scene: it is in fact Pierre, the painter's son, at the piano. But the subtle complexity of construction, the confusion of exchange between art and life that Matisse establishes, ensure that this family reference retains little of its literal meaning (unlike *The Music Lesson* of 1917, a more relaxed version of a similar theme exalting, in a simpler style, the happiness of the united family). *The Piano Lesson* is first of all a lesson in painting, which juxtaposes on the one surface, music, sculpture (*Decorative Figure*, 1908) and painting itself – by using a simplified representation of *Woman On Stool*, 1914, in such a way that she opens up the perspective space (even though that of the window is non-existent) whilst, at the same time, integrating the head of the young pianist.

Despite the importance of the verticals, the structure of the canvas is based on a series of corresponding triangular forms: the metronome is reversed on Pierre's face, and these two motifs are proportionally enlarged in the window. The piano itself is reduced to a simple three-dimensional shape, and the function of the arabesques of the balcony and partition-door is to counterbalance this geometric structure which, instead of attempting to reveal the intimate nature of objects and beings, as in Cubism, organizes the pictorial space in which these objects and beings can find their proper place, or in other words makes them accessible to the observers' view-point. It is remarkable that such accessibility, achieved entirely by 'the painting' itself, accords no more importance to the pianist than to the statuette or the woman painted in the state of suspension: art and life are invested with the same value, because only the former can permit any durable retention of the latter.

The Moroccans, 1916

181.3 × 279.4 cm. Museum of Modern Art, New York

This memory of Morocco, painted during the war, seems to answer the question of how a painting can recreate former happiness during a moment of collective crisis. It does so by representing two fragments from happier days against a background of disaster: the colour black fragments the image, insinuating itself between the forms, enclosing the coloured motifs which take on a sense of unhoped-for survival, all the more precious in that, despite their importance, we realize that they are about to be engulfed by the darkness.

Furthermore, the opposition of straight lines and curves brings a tension to the painting, a rigidity almost, corresponding in its own way to the strenuous effort Matisse must have maintained to depict happiness against all the odds. The quasi-abstraction of the figures, which has given rise to diverging interpretations (where Pierre Schneider sees a 'garden with pumpkins', Raymond Escholier discerns 'in the foreground, to the left, Moroccans at prayer, with orange head-dress and dressed in green'), underlines the fleeting nature of happy memories, which are nonetheless transfused into our perception. These, in turn, provide the painter with the opportunity to evoke, in a particularly nostalgic vein, a version of the Golden Age that he encountered in Tangier.

In a universe falling apart, heroism in painting consisted in an affirmation of the memory of former years in order to maintain the will to witness the return to happiness.

Bathers by a River, 1916

261.8 × 391.4 cm. Art Institute of Chicago

The final version of what was to become Shchukin's third panel, complementing *The Dance* and *Music*. Once again we have a paradisiacal theme – but, this time, it is paradise lost, despoiled by the insinuating presence of the serpent at the centre of the composition. Originally, the painting, begun in 1909, was painted in the same colours (green, blue and red) as the other panels. Matisse worked on it in parallel with the sculptures *Back I* and *Back II*, with which it shares a certain monumental quality and a tendency to treat the nude in an 'abstract' manner.

The background of the canvas, which consists of stylized foliage or parallel stripes, evokes no impression of fictive space: it exists entirely as a support for the figures which are themselves invested with a sanctifying rigidity; their outlines and specific definition give the effect of collage. The anonymity of the faces (already seen in *The Piano Lesson*, p.103, and becoming increasingly common in Matisse, see pp.121, 137) imbues them with a quality at once universal and dramatic, corresponding perfectly with the sculptural schematicism of the bodies. The muted scale of colours (once more due, perhaps, to the ambiance of the war years) accentuates the dramatization: when the profane world outside the studio is torn from its sacred origins as portrayed in *The Dance* (p.73), all that is left is in ruins, the inevitable spectacle of the Fall.

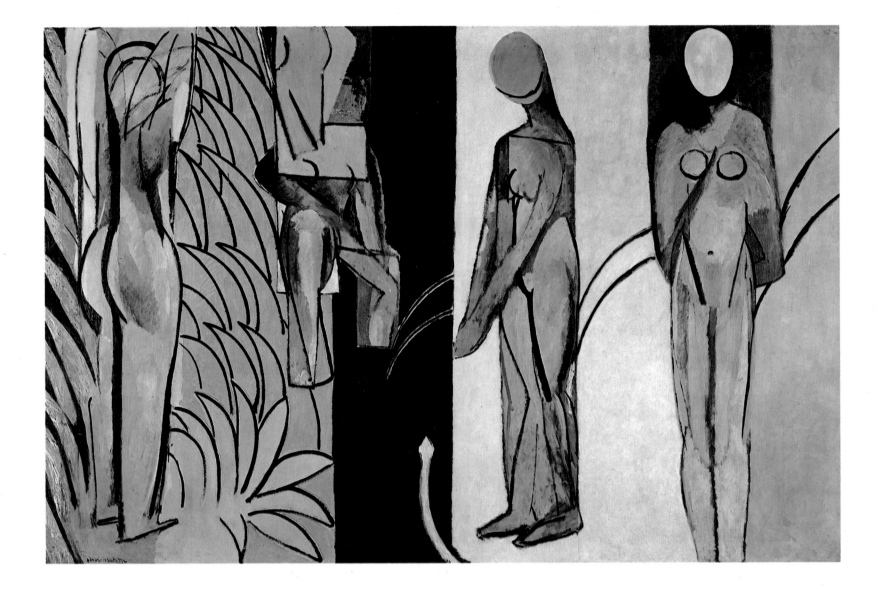

Auguste Pellerin II, 1916

150.2 × 92.6 cm. Musée national d'art Moderne, Paris

During the First World War, Matisse produced several portraits, as if to assemble around him elements of a humanity in grave danger, and to compensate for his anxiety about the survival of his family and friends.

This portrait of Auguste Pellerin was painted in two versions – a method Matisse was adopting more frequently (see pp.67, 73, 103, 121, 123). This one is the less realist of the two, and is executed in a narrower format than its counterpart, so that several elements can be removed (armchair and books in the background, ink-pot in front of the figure) from a decor which itself has been considerably modified, so that it now consists simply of the painting on the wall, and a closer focus on the model, who is consequently invested with a singularly powerful presence.

Once more, schematicism is at work, accentuating the lines of the face which the dark quarter-circle masking the painting brings into relief. It also gives a vigorous representation to the bust and the hands, and the look of the subject (much softer in the other version) is given an acuity paradoxically achieved by the asymmetric treatment of the eyes; while the desk exists only as a surface practically without perspective.

As, in these difficult years, it was often a case of 'putting on a bold front', the representation of the model could be considered as a *jeu de mots* underlined by the 'frontality' of the painting.

Coup de soleil, 1917

91 × 74 cm. Private collection

In his landscapes, Matisse frequently favoured locations with a natural slope, allowing him to take the horizon up to the top edge of the painting in order to draw the motif towards the pictorial plane. When he returned to the representation of nature in 1917, it is clear that he in no way abandoned the exigencies of geometric construction as this painting manifestly proves.

Coup de soleil (which indicates that Matisse must have seen the work of the Futurists) borders once more on the limits of non-figuration, in that the blocks of colour do not immediately evoke a pathway through the undergrowth – indicated only by two clearly recognizable trees. But the geometry and the tendency towards abstraction are entirely justified here by the theme, as in *French Window at Collioure*: they are determined by the vivid opposition between the brutal eruption of light through the leaves of the trees and the shadow this produces. The eye, initially dazzled, finds its transposition in the stark interruptions of colour and the bold transition from one to the other.

Interior with Violin, 1917–18

116 × 89 cm. Statens Museum for Kunst, Copenhagen

A first version of this piece presented an interior painted in mild tones, in delicate pinks and mauve. But Marguerite, the painter's daughter, declared that it was pretty: Matisse went straight back to work and set about introducing the tension that the painting now possesses.

The seclusion of the work-place (Matisse played the violin with a certain vigour) is broken by the eruption of the Mediterranean sunshine and an exterior world which reorientates the painting towards a realist point of view. The half-open blind forms an oblique which is continued in perspective by the window, and provides an opposition to the frontality of the violin-armchair arrangement. The illusory space reasserts its presence, solicited by the reality of a world with which reconciliation is possible (the return of peace). The mass of black no longer asserts itself as the colour of negation, but simply as a necessary function of light.

Once again the window plays its transitional role between the private world and the landscape (palm-tree, sand, sea): by allowing the light to enter, it puts these elements in communication with the interior. The intimate (the sentiment) and the visual are cross-fertilized.

Odalisque with Red Trousers, 1921

65 × 90 cm. Musée national d'art moderne, Paris

This is an example from the Odalisque series of the first Nice period, which brought Matisse under fire from critics who saw it as a painting without ambition. But this canvas demonstrates the painter's total mastery of the elaboration of space and his control of the decorative. The result is, beyond the reference to the female body, the construction of a painting equivalent to an imaginary theatre in which perspective, colours and subject are organized for the exaltation of life itself, presented in all its visual glory.

While the background is arranged into rigorous flat surfaces into which the divan introduces a bold perspective, the three-dimensional effects are reserved for the bust, with the red trousers taking on a quasi-frontality owing to the position of the legs, and are reinforced by the relationship established in yellow with the wall on the left. In this way the painting achieves its palpable and sensual unity; the decorative elements are balanced by the three dimensional quality of the flesh, while the uniformity of the floor maximizes the effect of the colour-scale, the sinuous lines of the body and the repeated motifs of the screens.

Decorative Figure on an Ornamental Background, 1925

131 × 98 cm. Musée national d'art moderne, Paris

In contrast to the previous *Odalisque With Red Trousers*, the first thing we notice here is the absence of any 'calm' zones: the canvas is a collection of decorative objects and motifs, which nevertheless retain a separate identity: the wallpaper is reminiscent of French baroque, the carpets are Persian, the mirror Venetian rococo, the flower-pot-holder from the Far East. An accumulative effect is thus created in relation to which the plant and the figure have difficulty in establishing themselves in a three-dimensional space, submitting more easily to the two-dimensional. By exaggerating the posture of the nude with the oblique of the right leg, and creating a sculptural effect by reducing the figure to a simplified arrangement of shapes (even if only one surface of the sculpture is represented), Matisse maintains a sense of perspective in the lower part of the painting. This perspective reappears in specific places when the eye focuses on the contiguity between the green leaves and the wallpaper bouquets. If, on the other hand, the eye moves toward the figure, the frontal view returns to embrace everything, including the carpet which can, in this case, be seen as a simple oblique motif.

This ambiguity gives the painting its force. The decorative (two-dimensional) and the realistic (three-dimensional) are opposed equally. We should note the absence of any reflection in the mirror and the latent agreement between the blue which covers it and that of the wallpaper: everything that would traditionally promote the illusion of perspective is drawn towards flatness. However, the sculptural figure itself, because of the unusual stiffness of the back, appears in some sense to displace the angle of the walls, which is absent in the background. Apart from the dazzling visual effect, these exchanges between the two directional pulls generate a tension which makes this painting an unquestionable masterpiece.

The Yellow Dress, 1929–31

100 × 81 cm. Baltimore Museum of Art

Painted for the most part in 1929, but finished two years later, *The Yellow Dress* is a comprehensive example of the new use of line in Matisse's painting (he was also drawing a lot at this time). The great variety (diagonals, verticals, the irregular contours of the tiles) breaks up the surface into areas which surround the central figure, whose dress defines the dominant colour and takes command of the painting. The half-opened blind paradoxically invests the interior with clarity: this time the window is a point of transition between two equal areas of light, exterior and interior.

The model's serene pose, simply drawn at the centre of the canvas, is in perfect harmony with the relaxed and calm atmosphere of the room. The mastery of colour is such that even the most daring combinations seem perfectly natural, unobtrusively taking their place in a painting whose apparent facility disguises its true audacity.

The Dance, 1931–32

340 × 387 cm; 355 × 498 cm; 333 × 391 cm. Musée national d'art moderne, Paris

The reappearance of the dance theme (see pp.61, 73, 87) in response to the Barnes Foundation commission – here we see the first version – gave Matisse the opportunity to return to an evocation of the Golden Age. Since this time, however, it was not a matter of painting, but of creating an 'architectural tableau', it would no longer be possible to continue the direction Matisse had pursued in the twenties. This commission accelerated the development of the work, making it necessary to simplify the figures, to make them universal rather than particular, 'to temper, if not exclude' what Matisse was to call 'the human element'. This meant that the emotional content had to be produced in an unusual manner. Matisse was no longer creating a painting for lovers of his work, but a mural for everybody. Hence the absence of the three-dimensional and of any allusion to perspective, since it was Matisse's intention to integrate his design into the wall that was to bear it as if it had always been there.

A preparatory study in pencil reveals the extent to which this dance was essentially a round, interrupted and transformed into the studied anonymity of exaggeratedly large figures (by truncating them Matisse invites the eye to follow the bodies across the surface of the paint). Their chromatic neutrality and the way in which mass is defined by only a few lines, increases their dynamism against the background, which is divided by three colours into a succession of areas separated by obliques. The monumental nature of the work is less a matter of actual dimensions than of implied ones – the 'virtual' prolongation of the bodies and the triangles which escape the restrictions of any limited format.

Window in Tahiti, 1935

226 × 172.7 cm. Cateau Museum

In 1939 Matisse accepted a commission for a cartoon for a Beauvais tapestry, in which he attempted to recreate 'the enchanted surroundings of Oceania'. In Tahiti he had taken photographs, sketching them in his hotel-room. These provided the basis for an engraving illustrating *Poésies* by Mallarmé (1931–32).

The first version, painted in oils (*Window in Tahiti*, Matisse Museum, Nice), is particularly rich in arabesques (the curtain and the trees) and plays with the three-dimensional through colour, both in the sea and in the elements of plant life. But Matisse was singularly disappointed with the finished tapestry and decided to attempt another version more suitable for weaving.

This second version in gouache is filled with flat, bright colour and contains important modifications which make – with the exception of the boat, the only indication of perspective – a strictly two-dimensional statement: all colour gradation has disappeared; the horizon has been raised; he has simplified the drawing, which in the upper half turns the clouds and hills into a unified mass, reduced the curtain into a flat motif, broadened the band representing the earth and the balustrades, which become simple blocks without relief, and altered the colour of the border on which the almond flowers are no longer outlined in black.

If *Window I* was more realist in its aims, *Window II* asserts the qualities of structure by horizontal registers, on which the motif acquires a superior intensity by virtue of the pure colours. Its decorative qualities confer on it an assertiveness which prefigures the gouache cut-ups.

Large Reclining Nude, 1935

65 × 92 cm. Baltimore Museum, Cone collection

Like *The Dream* painted in the same year, *Large Reclining Nude* seems, at first sight, to be perfectly simple, and one could be forgiven for thinking that its composition was accomplished with little difficulty. In fact this is far from the truth: it took five months to complete, including charcoal sketches, and photographs taken of the canvas at successive stages (published in Henri Matisse, 'L'Apparente Facilité' (Aimé Moeght, 1986), p.63 ff.) show that it underwent several re-workings, some traces of which are still visible. The original version was still relatively realist, giving some sense of the three-dimensional to the body and detailing the elements of the decor (the bouquet and the chair-back, which were finally reduced to extremely allusive forms). The checked material made its appearance progressively (initially in obliques). The position of the head was changed several times as was the relative importance of different parts of the body, originally submitted to a torsion which no longer remains in the definitive version of the painting.

The whole work, aiming for simplicity in its entirety, ultimately transforms the female body into a suggestion of form unattached to a specific person. There is nothing arbitrary about this form, in that it is the result of a process which has secretly nourished it: it is entirely convincing to the observer because it is a function of all the trial-runs which led to its completion. The painter experimented with it as the only possible form in the *ensemble* of the composition.

Nymph in the Forest, 1935–43

242 × 195 cm. Matisse Museum, Nice

The theme of this composition springs from the association of two elements: an etching done in 1931 to illustrate *Poésies* by Mallarmé, and sketches for a *Sleeping Nymph* realized in May and June, 1935. In September 1935, Matisse worked steadily on the canvas in charcoal, not dealing with colour until several months later. He realized that he was confining himself to 'the neo-impressionist colour-scale', but that his drawing was entirely self-referential, in pursuit of the single goal of his painting: 'to give a new, precious and varied quality to the surface'.

The painting was exhibited in May 1936 at the Rosenberg gallery: at the time it was surrounded by a border decked with garland motifs. In August, Matisse began work on it again, and was to come back to it periodically, making important modifications: the appearance of a central tree-trunk, the shortening of the stream, the relative effacement of the two figures and other forms, which were originally outlined, the neutralization of the border on which four almond flowers appear to the left (see *Window in Tahiti*, p.123).

This border now serves as a frame, as a window through which the scene is perceived, and in which the satyr's activity is indefinitely suspended. We should note that the recourse to mythology – favoured by recent illustrations to Mallarmé and Joyce – coincides indirectly with Tahiti: the two versions of the Golden Age are united, but at the same time seem to loose their vivacity. The painted and the non-painted combine to create a spectacle, but the spectacle is imprecise, as if shrouded in an oneiric mist.

The Romanian Blouse, 1940

92 × 73 cm. Musée national d'art moderne, Paris

Like the *Large Reclining Nude* (see p.125), this canvas, perhaps the most frequently reproduced of Matisse's works, was the result of an intensive work-period concentrating on simplification and the reduction of the whole to a collection of signs (face, blouse, embroidery), a period which lasted nine months. His departure-point was a rich floral decor with a bold motif, while the figure remained seated on the edge of a sofa; its significance in terms of the overall surface was originally less important.

The exaggeration of the sleeves ensures that the model dominate the whole surface and its fullness of form promotes it to the rank of a true archetype. It therefore became possible to reduce the intensity of the embroidery (at certain stages it covered the whole of the sleeves) because its representation, albeit incomplete, is invested with so much power that it stands out boldly from the red background and the blue skirt. Similarly, just the minimum of lines suffices to indicate the hair and face. The dislocation of the figure, originally a function of its seated position, becomes synonymous with gracefulness, the most appropriate way of occupying the available space.

'I have worked for years', Matisse admitted, 'in order that people might say: Matisse is only that!' The 'only that', meaning the purification of the motif, is only another way of describing an opulencce which overwhelms the perception of the observer.

Yellow and Blue Interior, 1946

116 × 81 cm. Musée national d'art moderne, Paris

The balance between areas of colour, the domination of the drawing and the harmony in this work create such a sense of assurance that it is easy to overlook its audacity. Nothing is quite 'normal', in a figuration which is nonetheless realist: the blue rectangle at the bottom is totally frontal (to the point where it could be interpreted as a painting leaning against the table); the table and the armchair suggest a sense of perspective which then disappears at the bottom of the canvas where the stool and the graphics on a blue background (a distant recollection of a Jouy painting) reaffirm the frontality. Colour invades every available space but is specifically placed only in certain objects (vase, lemons, water-melons). The furniture is treated only as a transparency, as if stripped of all matter (the table which served as a model had a marble top) to the point where the 'rocaille' armchair becomes, by virtue of its location, two-coloured. The light in the room, in which Matisse repeats the quadrangular form of the canvas itself, as a kind of double challenge to counterpoint the liberty of the curves inscribed within it, no longer needs to be defined: colour itself produces the painting's particular light.

Yellow and Blue Interior initiated a series of canvases (1946–48) in which Matisse resolves the conflict between colour and drawing by enabling them to exchange their traditional functions: here, in a space already saturated with colour, the black lines silhouette objects which assume an immediate accord with that which separates them. The surface of the canvas, worked with a lightness of application, becomes a continuum where the various plastic elements and signs exist in harmony.

130

Rocaille Armchair, 1946

92 × 73 cm. Matisse Museum, Nice

In April 1942, Matisse wrote to Aragon that he had 'finally found the object [he had] been seeking for more than a year. It is a baroque Venetian chair varnished with silver tints. Like an enamel . . . When I found it in an antique shop I was bowled over. It is splendid, I am possessed by it.' His enthusiasm for this object, which took its place alongside certain other favourite items (chairs for example) which he had collected over the years and which appear in canvas after canvas, immediately inspired several drawings, and even a sketch in oils in 1942. In this sketch, the armchair is represented in total perspective on a tiled floor, with the additional detail of some fruits and a vase.

The 1946 canvas takes on a majesty of altogether different proportions: for four years, the object has resided in the painter's imagination and sensibility. The overall form exceeds the surface area allotted to it as if the nobility attributed to it by Matisse can be only partially contained by the representation. The exaggeration of the motif in terms of the available pictorial space is an indication of its sanctification – but it is also the justification, thirty-eight years later, of the 'scandalous' comparison of 1908. It would appear that art is no longer even 'analogous to a good armchair' since the painting, this time, *is* an armchair – but it is simultaneously a harmony of colours, a dominant play of arabesques, and the evocation of a bouquet, all lightly applied to leave the supporting canvas visible, and, in their treatment, all equally capable of revealing the gestures which produced them.

Still Life with Grenadines, 1947

80 × 60 cm. Matisse Museum, Nice

After 1946, Matisse more or less consistently preferred representation without perspective. The window no longer opens the interior onto a broader landscape. The opposition between the two spaces is now indicated by other means, as this painting demonstrates. He uses colour (red-yellow-black for the interior, green-blue-white for the exterior) distributed according to shape: the coloured surfaces of the walls and the table, the circles of fruit and triangles of the curtain, counterbalance the green lines of the palm-leaves which lack any sense of a surface.

The narrow red blind affirms the existence of the window: in its absence, the clear rectangle could easily be interpreted as a painting hanging on the wall. Seen as a window, it indicates the existence of a bright light in the space outside. But this is not what justifies the dark walls (present in other works of the same period): in the two-dimensional canvas, the light does not produce shadows and the colours are chosen solely for reasons of internal harmony on the surface. The painting retains only the slenderest of links with its apparent subject matter: removed from illusionism, it becomes authentically metaphysical., To employ the well-known phrase uttered by Klee, whom Matisse described in a letter to Bonnard as a painter of rare sensitivity, it 'makes visible', that is to say, it gives the eye the opportunity to feast itself on forms and colours which are the genesis of things, the dawn of a universe free of all dross.

Blue Nude IV, 1952

103 × 74 cm. Matisse Museum, Nice

The series of four *Blue Nudes* (1952) assumes a special place amongst the gouache cut-ups – as much because of the exaltation of the quasi-monochrome as for the formal fullness of the sign, variously presented in the '*ensemble*': a female body in the same posture, left leg bent, foot caught in the compass of the right knee, right arm folded, almost touching the neck, head more or less inclined. The position of the legs represents a rotation through ninety degrees of their position in *Decorative Figure* (1925, see p.117).

Blue Nude IV is the result of a long succession of trial-runs, recorded in photographs. There is further evidence of these in the numerous charcoal marks which remain visible. In its finished state the painting offers a particularly supple image of the articulation of the limbs, with considerable importance attached to white.

If we remember that, for Matisse, to cut up gouache paper was to work directly with colour and material, we will notice that shapes are obtained by the juxtaposition and superimposition of fragments (in this case it took eleven to form the left thigh alone). Furthermore, the colour blue is not uniform; it presents at least three tonal values: the movement, the progressive adjustment of fragments, provided Matisse with a means of working directly with the surface of the representation, in a way not unlike sculpture, even though the image remains strictly two-dimensional.

A complete work of art, in which the sensual and intellectual experiences of the designer, colourist, sculptor and the architectural painter (cf. *The Dance*, p.121) are brought together, the gouache cut-up form must have seemed to Matisse to be the final achievement of his career. The decorative here asserts its unquestionable nobility and produces a monumental effect independent of the real format: the power of the figure is immeasurable.

Yellow Odalisque 1926

Renes.

Souvenir of Oceania, 1952–53

284.4 × 286.4 cm. Museum of Modern Art, New York

The elements (leaves, waves, flowers . . .) which evoke Oceania are quite common in the great gouache cut-up compositions. This one is entirely devoted to the 'memory', of a beach in Oceania: purified and transfigured by more than twenty years of meditation, it borders on the abstract. Nevertheless, we still recognize, on the right of the composition, the front end of a canoe and the characteristic curve of a palm-tree, while the yellow cut-up on the left indicates vegetation. These points of reference, with the help of lightly-traced charcoal lines, are sufficient to suggest a sense of the whole – which is primarily an articulation of coloured forms, arranged with such precision that the slightest displacement of a surface would disturb the harmony of the work.

Properly speaking, background does not exist in *Souvenir of Oceania* – the white is as active as the colours, which seem to emanate spontaneously from it. Matisse towards the end of his career revealed the possibility of a visual and sensual deployment in space, designed to overcome, enrapture and 'soothe' the observer: all references to previous forms of art have disappeared, the world as constituted by the painting is as pure as the air after a storm, lit by rays of unexpected sunshine.

SELECT BIBLIOGRAPHY

Writings by Matisse

Ecrits et Propos sur l'Art, edition annotated by Dominique Fourcade, Paris, Hermann Savoir collection, 1972.

Correspondance Matisse–Bonnard, Nouvelle Revue Française, numbers 211 and 212, July and August 1970.

Correspondance Matisse–Camoin, Revue de l'Art no. 12, 1971.

Writings on Matisse

ARAGON, Louis, *Henri Matisse, Roman*; Paris, Gallimand, 1971.

BARR, Alfred, *Matisse, his Art and his Public*, New York Museum of Modern Art, 1951.

BESSON, Georges, *Matisse*, Paris, éditions Braun, collection des Maîtres, 1954; *Cahiers Henri Matisse*, Henri Matisse Museum, Nice; 5 volumes (1: *Matisse et Tahiti*; 2: *Matisse, photographies*; 3: *Matisse, L'Art du Livre*; 4: *Matisse, Ajaccio, Toulouse*; 5: *Matisse, aujourd'hui*; *Henri Matisse*, Paris, Georges Crès, 1920; *Hommage à Henri Matisse*, Paris, XXth century, 1970; *Nouvelle Revue Française* no. 211, July 1970, Paris, Gallimard; *Critique* no 234, May 1974, Paris, éditions de Minuet. *Henri Matisse, Paper Cut-Outs*, Saint Louis Museum and Detroit Institute of Art, 1977; *Tout l'oeuvre peint de Henri Matisse, 1904–26*, Paris, Flammarion, 1982.

DELECTORSKAYA, Lydia, *L'Apparente Facilité . . . Henrry Matisse*, Paris, Adrien Maeght, 1986.

DIEHL, Gaston, *Matisse*, Paris, Tisné, 1954.

DUTHUIT-MATISSE, Marguerite and DUTHUIT, Georges, *Henri Matisse: l'Oeuvre Gravé*, Paris, 1983.

DUTHUIT, Georges, *Henri Matisse; Livres Illustrés*, Paris, 1983.

ESCHOLIER, Raymond, *Matisse, Ce Vivant*, Paris, Librairie A. Fayard, 1956.

FERRIER, Jean-Louis, *Matisse, 1911–30*, Paris, Fernand Hazan, 1961.

FLAM, Jack, *Matisse, the Man and his Art, 1869–1918*, Cornell University Press, Ithaca and London, 1986.

FRY, Roger, *Henri Matisse*, Paris, Editions des Chroniques du Jour, 1935.

GUICHARD-MEILI, Jean, *Matisse, les Gouaches Découpées*, Paris, Fernand Hazan, 1983; *Henri Matisse*, Paris, Somogy, 1988.

LASSAIGNE, Jacques, *Matisse*, Geneva, Skira, 1959.

NOËL, Bernard, *Matisse*, Paris, Fernand Hazan, collection 'Les Maîtres de l'Art', 1987.

PLEYNET, Marcelin, 'Le système de Matisse' in *L'Enseignement de la Peinture*, Paris, Editions de Seuil, 1971; *Qui êtes-vous? Henri Matisse*, Lyon, La Manufacture, 1988.

RUSSEL, John, *Matisse and his Time*, Time-Life, 1973.

SCHNEIDER, Pierre, *Matisse*, Paris, Flammarion, 1984.

SELZ, Jean, *Henri Matisse*, Paris, Flammarion, 1964.

SEMBAT, Marcel, *Henri Matisse*, Paris, Editions de la Nouvelle Revue Française, 'Les peintres Français Nouveaux', collection, 1920.

VERDET, André, *Prestiges de Matisse*, Paris, Editions Emile-Paul, 1952.

Principle Exhibition Catalogues

Henri Matisse, les grandes gouaches découpées, Paris, Musée des arts décoratifs, 1961.

Henri Matisse. Retrospective, Los Angeles, University of California Press, 1966.

Henri Matisse. Exposition du Centenaire, Paris, Grand Palais, 1970.

Matisse au Musée de Grenoble, Grenoble, Musée des beaux arts, 1975.

Matisse. Catalogue des Collections du Musée national d'art moderne, Paris, Centre Georges Pompidou, 1979.

Henri Matisse. The Early Years in Nice, National Gallery of Art, Washington, Harry N. Abrams, New York, 1986.

Matisse. Peintures et Dessins du Musée Pouchkine et du Musée de l'Ermitage, Lille, Musée des beaux arts, 1986.

Matisse, Venice, Correr Palace, 1987.

Matisse. Le Rythme et la Ligne, Paris, Ecole nationale supérieure des beaux arts, 1987.

Henri Matisse. Autoportraits, Le Cateau, Musée Matisse, 1988.

PHOTOGRAPH CREDITS

Succession Henri Matisse: 6, 22, 23, 28, 29, 73. Flammarion: 8, 47, 51, 55, 61, 63, 65, 69, 71, 75, 77, 79, 81, 83, 85, 87, 97, 99, 103, 107, 111, 113, 119, 121. Steichen, Réunion des Musées Nationaux: 15. Bibliothèque National: 16, 18, 19, 26, 36, 37. Magnum, Robert Capa: 25. Henri Cartier-Bresson: 30, 31, 39. Helen Adant: 33. Musée Matisse, Nice: 45, 49, 123, 133, 135, 137. Musée national d'art moderne, Paris: 53, 67, 93. Musée de Grenoble: 59. Réunion des Musées Nationaux: 91. Museum of Modern Art, New York: 101, 139. Photo C H Bahier, P H Migeat: 109, 115, 117, 131. Museum of Baltimore: 125. Other photographs are from the editor's collection.

CHRONOLOGY

1869
Henri Matisse born, December 31st, Cateau-Cambrésis. Childhood spent in Bohain, Picardy.

1883–87
Pupil at the Saint-Quentin lycée.

1887–88
Student of law in Paris. The next year he returns to Saint-Quentin as a solicitor's clerk. He attends courses in applied drawing.

1890
During a long convalescence he starts to paint, copying lithographs and using a paint-box given as a present by his mother.

1891–94
Enrols at Académie Julien in Paris; studies with Gustave Moreau in his Fine Arts studio: here he meets Marquet and Manguin. Frequent visits to the Louvre to make copies.

1895
Lives at 19, quai Saint Michel. First trip to Brittany.

1896
Takes part in the Salon de la Société nationale des Beaux Arts (elected associate member). Second trip to Brittany: here Russell introduces him to Van Gogh.

1897
Third trip to Brittany. Negative reaction to *The Dinner Table* at the Salon. Meets Pissaro and Camoin.

1898
Marriage to Amélie Parayre; honeymoon in London where he studies Turner. Discovers the south of France and its particular light (Corsica, Toulouse, Perpignan). Death of Gustave Moreau.

1899
Birth of his first son Jean. Buys a Cézanne from the dealer Vollard (*Trois Baigneuses*), also a Rodin plaster, a Van Gogh drawing and a small Gauguin canvas. Continues outdoor painting in Paris and Arcuil. He takes evening classes in sculpture.

1900
Birth of his second son, Pierre. To support his family he works with Marquet on the decoration of the Grand Palais for the Universal Exhibition.

1901
After an illness, convalescence in the Swiss Alps: the grandeur of the Alps did not inspire him to paint. Exhibits at the Salon des Indépendants. Derain introduces him to Vlaminck. Takes part in an exhibition of former students of Moreau at the gallery owned by Berthe Weill – who sold his first painting.

1903
Exhibits at Berthe Weill's gallery, at the Indépendants and at the first Salon d'Automne. Produces his first engravings and finishes his sculpture *Le Serf*.

1904
First one-man exhibition at the Vollard gallery (46 paintings, foreword by Roger Marx). Spends the summer at Saint Tropez with Signac; he meets Félix Fénéon.

1905
Exhibits *Luxe, calme et volupté* at the Indépendants; the painting is acquired by Signac. Summer at Collioure. Here he meets Maillol and Daniel de Monfreid, who leads him to a better understanding of Gauguin. The 'Cage aux Fauves' scandal at the Salon d'Automne. First purchase by the Steins (*Woman with Hat*) and by Marcel Sembat. Beginnings of success.

1906
One-man exhibition at the Druet gallery (55 paintings). Exhibits only one canvas at the Indépendants, *La Joie de vivre* purchased by Léo Stein. Trip to Algeria and a stay at Collioure. Discovers *art nègre*. Meets Picasso at the Steins' apartment.

1907
Apollinaire's article in *La Phalange*. *Blue Nude* shown at the Indépendants. First visit to Italy, then another stay at Collioure. *Le Luxe I* exhibited at the Salon d'Automne. Encouraged by Sarah Stein and Hans Purrmann to set up an *académie* in the rue de Sèvres.

1908
Academy and studio in the boulevard des Invalides. First exhibition in New York. Trip to Bavaria. Publishes *Notes d'un Peintre* in *La Grande Revue*. *Red Dining Table* purchased by Schukine.

1909
Rents a large house in Issy les Moulineaux which he was to buy three years later; here he constructed a studio to facilitate work on the two panels commissioned by Schukine (*The Dance* and *Music*). Gradually phases out his teaching obligations in boulevard des Invalides. First contract for the Bernheim-Jeune gallery thanks to Fénéon.

1910
First retrospective at the Bernheim-Jeune gallery. Visit to an exhibition of moslem art in Munich. Seco,d version of *The Dance* and *Music* exhibited at the Salon d'Automne. Leaves for Spain.

1911
Works in Seville; returns in the spring to Issy (*The Red Studio*), then

goes back to Collioure. Trip to Moscow where he takes an interest in the icons. Stays in Tangier until the spring of 1912.

1912

First sculpture exhibition. Return to Tangier in December.

1913

United States: takes part in the Armory Show through which the American public discovers different trends in modern art: in Chicago, the *Blue Nude* of 1907 creates a scandal. Moroccan paintings shown at the Bernheim-Jeune: Morosov purchases the *Moroccan Triptych*. Rents another studio on the quai Saint Michel.

1914

Summer in Collioure (*French Window at Collioure*), where he meets Juan Gris. Alfred C. Barnes begins purchasing numerous works, as do Danish collectors.

1915

Exhibition in New York.

1916

Paris and Issy (*The Moroccans*, *The Piano Lesson*). First stay in Nice, Beau Rivage hotel.

1917

Issy, Paris, Nice. Visits Renoir.

1918

Matisse-Picasso exhibition at the Paul Guillaume gallery (foreword by Apollinaire). Rents an apartment in Nice. Visits Bonnard in Antibes.

1919

Exhibitions at the Bernheim-Jeune and in London.

1920

Décor and costumes for *Le Chant du Rossignol* by Stravinsky and Massine, presented by Diaghliev's Russian Ballet.

1921

From now on divides his time between Paris and Nice. *Odalisque with Red Trousers* purchased by the Luxembourg Museum.

1922

Madame Marguerite Matisse makes a donation of *Interior with Aubergines* to the Grenoble Museum.

1923

Marcel Sembat bequest to the Grenoble Museum. In Moscow the foundation of the Museum of Western Modern Art with the collections of Schukine and Morosov.

1924

Retrospective in Copenhagen. Exhibitions in New York and at the Bernheim-Jeune.

1925

Trip to Italy (Naples and Sicily), *Decorative Figure on an Ornamental Background*.

1927

Receives the Carnegie Prize.

1930

Finishes *Back IV*. Trip to Tahiti via New York and San Francisco. On the jury of the Carnegie Prize (awarded to Picasso). At the end of the year, returns to the United States: Dr. Barnes commissions Matisse to do large-scale decorative work for his foundation.

1931

Retrospectives in Paris, Basle and New York. Works on the illustrations for Mallarmé's *Poésies* and *The Dance* for Barnes.

1932

Due to an error in dimensions given, Matisse is obliged to work on a second version of *The Dance* for Barnes.

1933

Trip to Merion in order to supervise the installation of *The Dance*. Medical treatment in Venice; reviews the Giottos in Padua.

1934

Exhibition at his son Pierre's home in New York.

1935

Cartoons for tapestries (*Window in Tahiti*). Beginning of collaboration with Lydia Delectorskaya.

1937

Exhibition at the Rosenberg gallery. Commission from Massine for décor and costumes for the ballet *Rouge et Noir*. The museum of the Ville de Paris acquires the first version of Barnes' *The Dance*.

1938

The Luxembourg museum purchases *Decorative Figure on an Ornamental Background*. Moves into the former Hotel Regina in Cimiez.

1939

Summer in the Hotel Lutétia in Paris. Goes to see the Prado paintings in Geneva; returns to Nice in October.

1940

Leaves for Bordeaux after the fall of Paris. Cancels a trip to Brazil. Returns to Nice in October. *The Romanian Blouse*.

1941

In January, a serious operation in Lyon: Matisse recovers; the sisters from the clinic call him 'le Ressuscité'. Back in Paris he begins painting from his bed.

1942

Aragon visits Cimiez. Several drawings: *Thèmes et Variations*. Attacks contemporary academism over the radio. Communication and exchange of paintings with Picasso. Illustrations for *Poèmes* by Charles d'Orléans.

1943

Moves to Vence, villa 'Le Rêve'. Retrospective in New York at the home of Pierre Matisse.

1944

Madame Matisse imprisoned and Marguerite Matisse-Duthuit arrested as resistance members. Begins the gouache cut-ups which will become *Jazz*. Illustrations for *Les Fleurs du Mal*.

1945

Exhibition in London with Picasso. Retrospective at the Salon d'Automne. Recent canvases, accompanied by photographs showing their various stages of development exhibited at the Aimé Maeght gallery.

1946

Illustrations for *Lettres d'une religieuse portugaise* and *Visages* by Reverdy.

1947

Jazz appears at the Tériade gallery. Important works take their place in the newly-opened Musée national d'art moderne.

1947

Publication of *Florilège des Amours de Ronsard*, illustrated with 126 lithographs. Works on the Chapelle de Vence project and on the large gouache cut-ups. A touring exhibition in the United States.

1949

Back to the Hotel Régina. Exhibitions in New York (Pierre Matisse gallery), Paris (Musée national d'art moderne) and Lucerne (retrospective).

1950

Publication of *Poèmes* by Charles d'Orléans. Sculptures and maquettes for the Vence chapel (Maison de la Pensée française, Paris, foreword by Aragon). Laureate of the XXVth Venice biennale, sharing the prize with Henri Laurens.

1951

Inauguration of the Chapelle de Vence. Gouache cut-ups, but also a return to painting for the first time in three years. Exhibitions in Japan and New York.

1952

Inauguration of the Matisse Museum in Cateau: the initial selection and presentation controlled by Matisse. *Blue Nude* series in gouache cut-ups.

1953

Exhibition of paper cut-ups at the Berggruen gallery. Sculptures in London and New York.

1954

Matisse dies of a heart attack on 3rd November.

LIST OF PLATES